Book 1 in this series: **"Delaware Before the Railroads"**
Book 3 in this series: **"Delaware from Freeways to e-Ways"**
Coming soon!

"Delaware from Railways to Freeways"
Published by Dave Tabler
www.davetabler.com

Printed in the United States of America

ISBN 979-8-9870006-3-2
Library of Congress Control Number: 2023911764

Cover Design: Onur Burç

Acknowledgments

Many organizations offered their support to the development of this book. Heartfelt thanks to (in alphabetical order) Bombay Hook National Wildlife Refuge, Bowers Beach Maritime Museum, Camden Friends Meetinghouse, Camden Parks Department, Delaware Agricultural Museum and Village, Delaware Public Archives, Delaware Historical & Cultural Affairs, Delaware Historical Society, Delaware Society for the Preservation of Antiquities, Delaware Tourism Office, DNREC Division of Fish and Wildlife, Captain Donald Deputy, Duck Creek Historical Society, First State National Historical Park, Friends of Old Dover, Inc., Free Library of Philadelphia, Friends of Old Swedes, Friends of Zoar, Inc., Georgetown Historical Society, Greater Harrington Historical Society, Hagley Museum & Library, Regina Higgins, Historic Odessa Foundation Inc., Johnson Victrola Museum, Knowles Museum, Lewes Historical Society, Marvel Carriage Museum, Milford Historical Society, Milford Museum, National Park Service, Nemours Estate, New Bedford Whaling Museum, New Castle Historical Society, Old Courthouse - Georgetown Historical Society, Charmaine Pardee, Pencader Heritage Museum, Presbyterian Historical Society, Seaford Museum, Heather Straub, Smithsonian Institution, Smyrna Museum, St. Jones Center for Estuarine Studies, Dr. Kenneth A. Tabler, National Postal Museum, Winterthur Museum Garden & Library, Zwaanendael Museum.

Preface

The advent of the railroad ushered in a prosperous era for the First State. Delaware boasts a strategic location along the easily navigable Delaware Bay. This unique geographical advantage facilitates efficient cargo distribution to a myriad of ports throughout the mid-Atlantic region. Thriving industries established themselves along these bustling waterways, from which they could ship goods to nearby urban centers such as Philadelphia.

The early 19th century arrival of the New Castle & Frenchtown Railroad prompted a significant shift from sea to land transport. Two decades later, the Delaware Railroad dropped like a plumb line through the center of the state, creating 'whistle stop' towns such as Clayton, Wyoming, and Felton. The rail network hastened the transport of farm produce and ripened fruit, enabling farmers and orchardists to access major markets before spoilage. Large scale production blossomed, fostering a sense of regional pride and satisfaction.

Sailing ships built in Delaware continued to navigate ocean waters, but locally constructed steam-powered vessels gained importance, and finally dominance. The demand for the latter spurred the growth of iron shipyards in Wilmington. The town of Bethel, meanwhile, developed the specialized schooner Chesapeake Ram.

DuPont emerged during the era's early industrial expansion, establishing an explosive-manufacturing facility in the Brandywine Valley. The U.S. Government sought it out for gunpowder supplies in both the Mexican and Civil Wars.

The War Between the States precipitously disrupted all this progress. Delaware's border state status in the conflict led to a bitter split, pitting brother against brother. Despite its allegiance to the Union, Delaware supplied between 3,000 to 4,000 soldiers in support of the Confederacy.

"Delaware from Railways to Freeways" encapsulates all this expansive history and more. Ultimately, the volume's narrative arc culminates in the advent of the automobile.

The book's structure presents a thorough and captivating pictorial history. Guided by meticulously selected photographs, vibrant illustrations, and informative captions, readers have the option to explore further through extended accounts found in the "Notes on Photographs" section. Sidebars add a touch of local flavor, highlighting unique 19th-century Delaware traditions.

Both casual readers and aficionados will value the exploration through Delaware's vibrant history. Noteworthy personalities, along with their challenges and triumphs, are duly acknowledged. Their endeavors, amplified by the state's inherent geographical advantages, played a significant role in sculpting Delaware's distinct identity.

My hope, dear reader, is that the formative years of Delaware remain relevant and celebrated.

\

Contents

1800-1825 Beginnings

1826-1850 Iron & Rails

1851-1875 Civil War & Reconstruction

1876-1907 The Gilded Age & Beyond

Customs & Folklore Sidebars

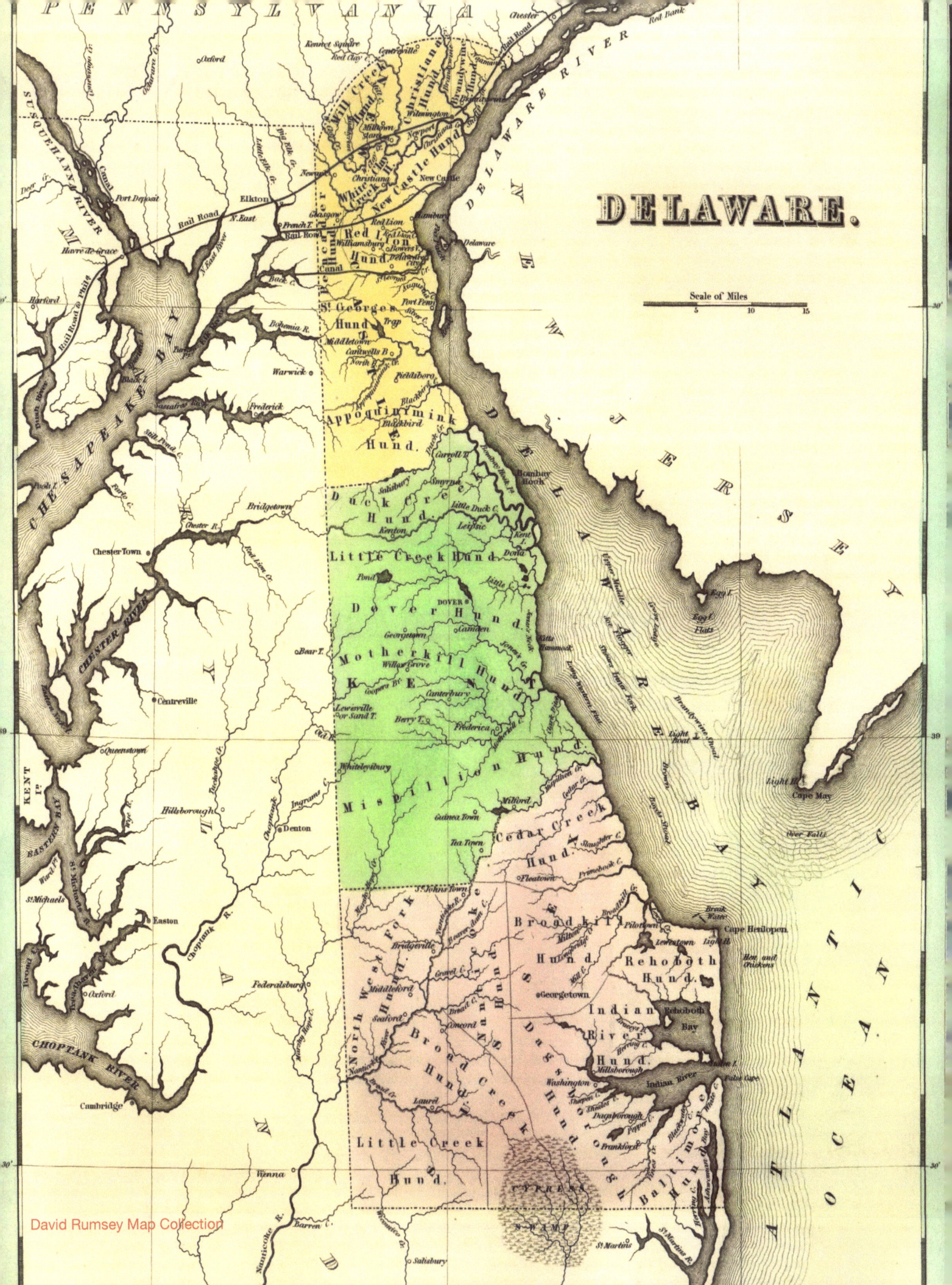

DELAWARE.

Scale of Miles
5   10   15

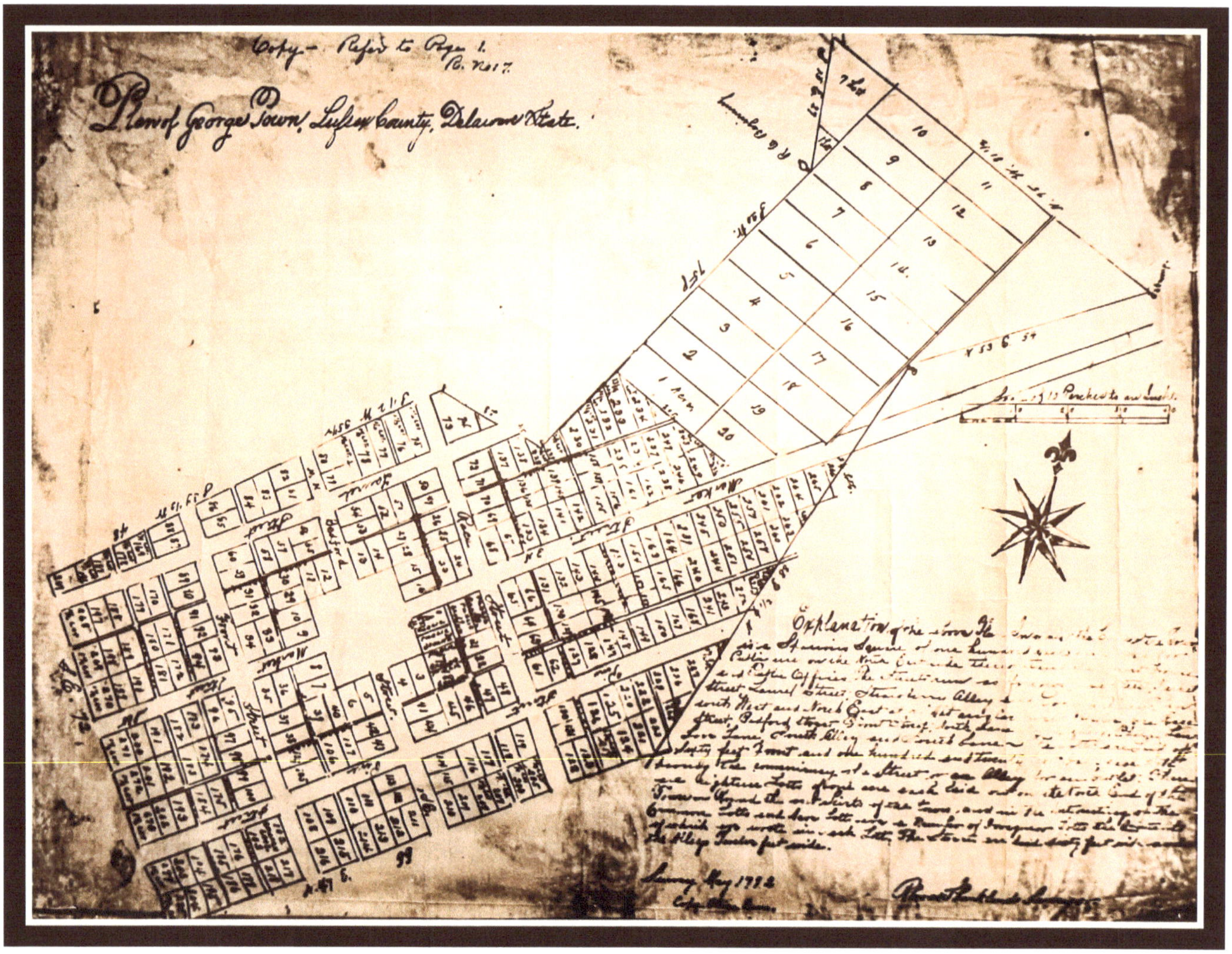

Rhoad Shankland, skilled lawyer and surveyor, is predominantly known for his work in platting Georgetown, widely regarded as one of the best-designed towns in Sussex County. His 1792 town plan, displayed above, showcases expertise in the field. In particular, Shankland utilized the compass depicted on the left to design a beautiful circular park at the town center, intended "for publick use." However, there is more to this public servant than his town planning. (cont. on pg. 77)

Return Day

Sussex County takes unique pride in a distinctive political tradition known as Return Day. The custom occurs on the Thursday following an election. Festivities include parades, celebrations, and other forms of revelry. However, Return Day was not always a lighthearted affair. In fact, the practice originated as a response to the political tensions and violence erupting during the 1787 election. The Tories and the Whigs aimed to prevent such conflicts in the future. (cont. on pg. 77)

Envision the emblematic Conestoga wagon, synonymous with early American history. One might associate these wagons with the Oregon Trail, which is often characterized by a parade of 'prairie schooners' journeying across the Kansas territory. In actuality, the wagon derives its name from Pennsylvania's Conestoga River. It was there that German immigrants encountered the Native American tribe known as the Conestoga or Susquehannock.

The widespread use of the wagon, primarily designed for freight transportation rather than pioneer conveyance, extended into Delaware. Its contoured design promoted cargo stabilization, preventing items from sliding off when navigating mountain inclines (or, considering Delaware's topography, gentle slopes!). During their zenith, more Conestogas passed in and out of New Castle daily than through any other landing sites in Delaware. (cont. on pg. 78)

In the 19th century, bald cypress trees were a valuable resource for residents of Sussex County, providing insect and water-resistant lumber that was well-suited for outdoor use. This versatile wood was utilized for a variety of purposes, ranging from water pipes to coffins. The trees' large, straight trunks yielded easily split wood which was ideal for creating roofing shingles and comparable siding. If you come across an old house in Delaware with a silver-gray bald cypress roof covered in moss, like the one depicted to the right, it's a telltale sign the structure was constructed during the 18th or 19th century. Below, a stand of bald cypress in Trap Pond State Park. (cont. on pg. 77)

Decoy Ducks

Collectors worldwide seek intricately carved decoy ducks depicting renowned Delaware birds such as the canvasback, brant, and mallard. The decoy duck industry emerged during the early 19th century in conjunction with the advent of steamboats and punt guns (massive shotguns often measuring between 8-10 feet long with up to 2-inch bores). (cont. on pg. 78)

The tale of George Washington chopping down a cherry tree and confessing to the act first appeared in M.L. Weems' well-known biography. Delaware remembers Weems as a colorful character with a penchant for storytelling. (cont. on pg. 78)

M.L. Weems once preached at St. Peters, in Lewes.

from heaven, brighter than the sun, ...mpanions. When we had all fallen ...ring to me in the Hebrew langua... ...ng me?' It hurts you to kick again... ...d stand on you... time; for it is not you who speak, but the S... speaking through you. Brother will betra... father his child, and children will rise a... put to death, and you will be hated b... the one who endures to the end w...

The Manby Mortar, unlike guns designed to take lives, was created to save lives. This maritime device, invented by Captain George Manby (1765-1854), fired a specially crafted life-saving cannonball attached to a line from the shore onto the deck of a nearby sinking ship. The survivors' rescue team, racing against time, secured the other end of the hawser to a small lifeboat. As they paddled towards the sinking ship, the lifeboat's coxswain simultaneously pulled the line, drawing the boat closer to those in distress. The etching illustrates the mortar's inaugural use in 1808, rescuing the "Elizabeth" off the coast of Great Yarmouth, England. The Manby Mortar depicted here was used for many years by the Indian River Life Saving Station. Rockets superseded the Manby Mortar by the late 1800s. Their range was longer; they were more accurate, and generally safer to use. The replacement, nonetheless, maintained the basic principle of launching a line to a distressed ship. *Collection Zwaanendael Museum*

Covered Bridges

Older covered bridges are designed to protect their structural integrity. The covering, or "house," shields the wood construction from rain, snow, ice and sun. Delaware originally possessed 35 covered bridges. This number decreased to 13 by 1868, further dwindling to only 5 by 1937, and currently standing at just 3. The remaining bridges, all situated in Wilmington, include from top to bottom, Wooddale Bridge, Ashland Bridge, and Smith's Bridge. Recurring flood damage, fires, and wood deterioration pose a constant threat to these historic structures. (cont. on pg 79)

Samuel Warren's Fleatown Inn earned a reputation for raucous partying in the early 19th century. Stagecoach travelers traversing the Milford and Georgetown corridor were grateful to have a halfway point to rest. Fleatown existed solely as a convenient stop between the two popular destinations. This small settlement, located on Old State Road in Broadkill Hundred, was essentially just a wide spot in the road. The distance between Milford and Georgetown, approximately 16 miles as the crow flies, was a significant journey. Before railways or automobiles, the only option was a two-day trip on dusty, rutted tracks weaving through underbrush teeming with mosquitoes.

Oh—then there was the goose that 'tended bar.' (cont. on pg. 79)

Opposite page: Solomon Bayley trembled for his life. Two slave hunters walked straight toward the thicket where he had spent the night. "I was struck with dread, and afraid to move hand or foot," he thought to himself. (cont. on pg. 80)

"A large fallen tree provided a hiding place."

Residents of New York City who relish the pure waters of the Croton River in upstate New York owe their access, in part, to southern Delaware. Foundries in this area produced the iron pipes crucial for the initial delivery of those waters during the early 19th century. The bog iron ore found along Delaware's Nanticoke River and its numerous branches also supplied iron for the railings at Philadelphia's Independence Square. These abundant deposits helped establish Sussex County as an early industrial center, although the county's iron industry thrived for only 50 years. (cont. on pg. 80)

Communion Tokens

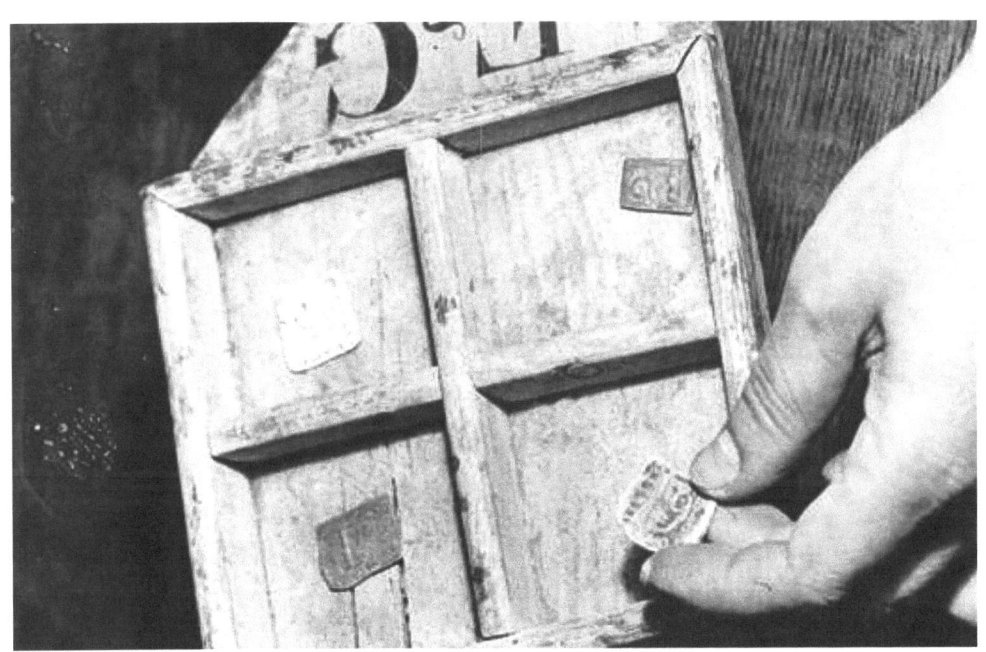

Delaware's Presbyterian churches used "communion tokens" until around 1860 to demonstrate one's good standing within the church. This communion practice, originally introduced by John Calvin in 1560, aimed to prevent the profanation of the Lord's Table. To receive a token, members had to demonstrate their knowledge of the faith and their adherence to the church's moral standards. The token system was a tangible method of enforcing discipline. Receipt of a token was usually determined through a process of examination by the church elders. If a member was found to be in good standing, they were given a token, which they would then present before communion. (cont. on pg. 81)

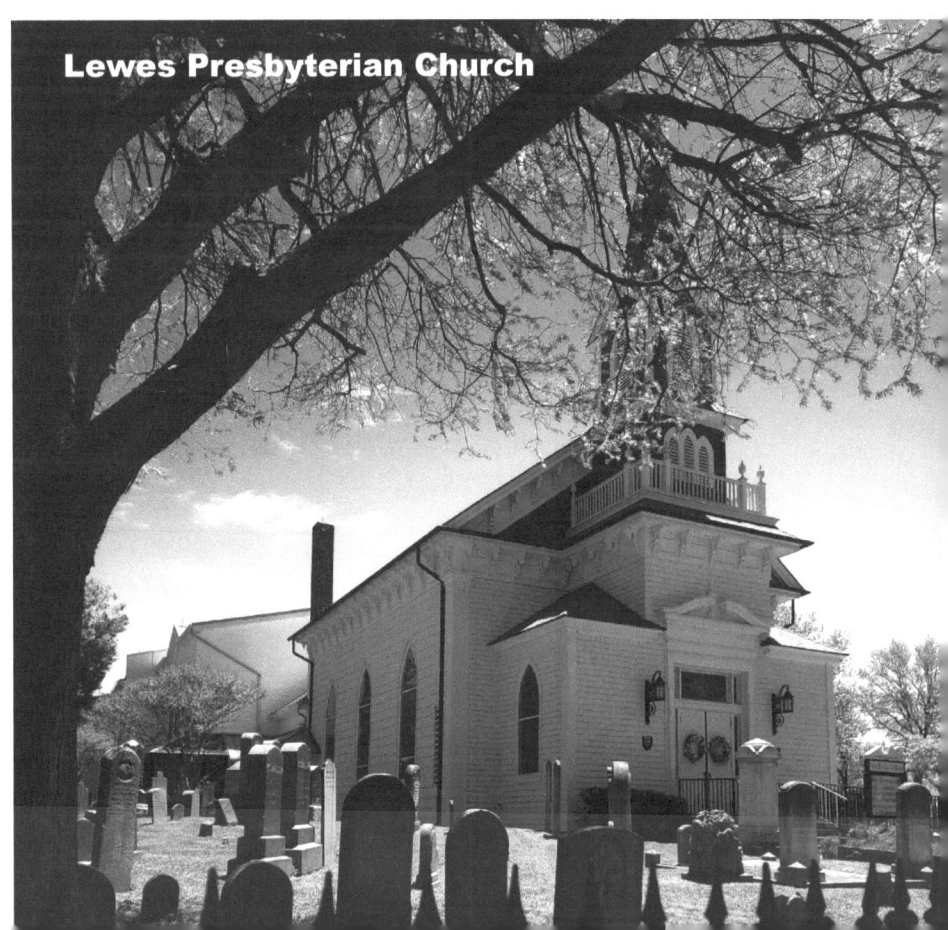

Lewes Presbyterian Church

Was an arsenic vial hidden in this secret compartment? (cont. on pg. 81)

Jacob Cannon operated a prosperous ferry business for many years on the Nanticoke River between Woodland and Laurel (below). Cannon constructed this magnificent new home (right) for his soon-to-be wife near the Woodland terminus. However, the young lady failed to appear on their wedding day, leaving him distraught. Cannon locked the door and simply walked away. The house remained unoccupied until his passing, 23 years later. The empty structure stared forlornly day after day at the bachelor, as he traversed his ferry route back and forth. Jacob Cannon's bizarre reaction to his unfortunate predicament resonates with the story of eccentric Miss Havisham from Charles Dickens' "Great Expectations." Dickens relates how a young woman has bedecked her

home for a glorious wedding day. The guests have all arrived; the table is covered in lace and the centerpiece features a tiered wedding cake. The appointed time for the ceremony comes...but the bridegroom does not show up. Miss Havisham continues to live in the house, wears her wedding dress, and leaves the wedding decorations exactly as they were...frozen in that moment forever. (cont. on pg. 82)

Nearly 200 merchant ships sank in Delaware Bay (1810-1826) as a result of violent storms and ice floes. Delaware, New Jersey, and Pennsylvania jointly implored the federal government to address the escalating calamities. *The Wilmingtonian and Delaware Advertiser* conceded that "Constructing a breakwater will be costly and challenging, but its benefits will outweigh the costs, considering the annual suffering of seamen and the loss of property due to the absence of proper shelter near the Delaware Bay coast." The Delaware Breakwater, constructed from 1829 to 1835, was one of the earliest national public works projects. Some states resented the choice of Delaware ahead of their similar large-scale projects. **Right:** Bellevue Quarry in New Castle County supplied the granite blocks for the project. (cont. on pg. 82)

The New Castle and Frenchtown Rail Road (ticket booth, left) epitomizes mechanical engineering's evolution. Observe the section of the New Castle, DE terminus below, and consider the railroad ties' absence. Established as Delaware's inaugural railroad, the NC&F was also one of the earliest nationwide. Its right of way mirrored the New Castle and Frenchtown Turnpike, a vital stagecoach route across the Delmarva peninsula's northern part since 1816, linking Baltimore and Philadelphia markets via steamboat ports. By the 1820s, stagecoaches hauling north-south travelers had become a lucrative enterprise in the region. The NC&F's investors foresaw profit in elevating their stagecoach wheels onto a track, enabling their horse-drawn hackneys to outpace rivals.(cont. on pg. 83)

The Wilmington Whaling Company (WWC), Delaware's only whaling venture, operated from 1833 to 1846, marking it as one of few such enterprises outside New England. A group of prominent Wilmington bankers and businessmen launched this venture in late 1833, pooling a capital stock of $100,000. Captain Richard Weeden set sail for the Pacific on the *Ceres* in May 1834, embarking on a three-year journey. The following year, in 1835, WWC sought corporate status and outlined ambitious plans for expansion. The venture aimed to construct ten ships and establish a factory for candle making and sperm oil processing. WWC successfully gained its charter and raised an additional $300,000 shortly thereafter. (cont. on pg. 83)

Below: Bayard Berndt, *Wilmington Riverfront circa 1880*, oil (painted from Market Street at the Christina Riverfront in Wilmington). Courtesy Hardcastle Galleries.

Sperm Whaleing

Left: The Old College, oldest building at the University of Delaware. Francis Alison, a highly educated Scotch-Irish emigrant, arrived in colonial America around 1735. He spent the next nine years establishing himself within the Presbyterian hierarchy. Alison developed relationships with other ministers and community members, as well as serving in various roles within church circles. He went on to play a significant lead in the early years of Presbyterianism and that denomination's quest for educational prominence. The University of Delaware owes a debt of gratitude to Francis Alison, a visionary, purpose-driven leader. (cont. on pg. 84)

William Huffington established The *Delaware Register and Farmer's Magazine* in February 1838, marking the inception of the state's first monthly magazine. This publication sought to offer valuable information and assistance to farmers. Rural inhabitants grappling with weather issues, soil conditions and pests also found it helpful. Moreover, the Dover-based journal featured articles on local history and education. Given the significance of agriculture to Delaware's early economy, the content aimed to cater to community needs. (cont. on pg. 84)

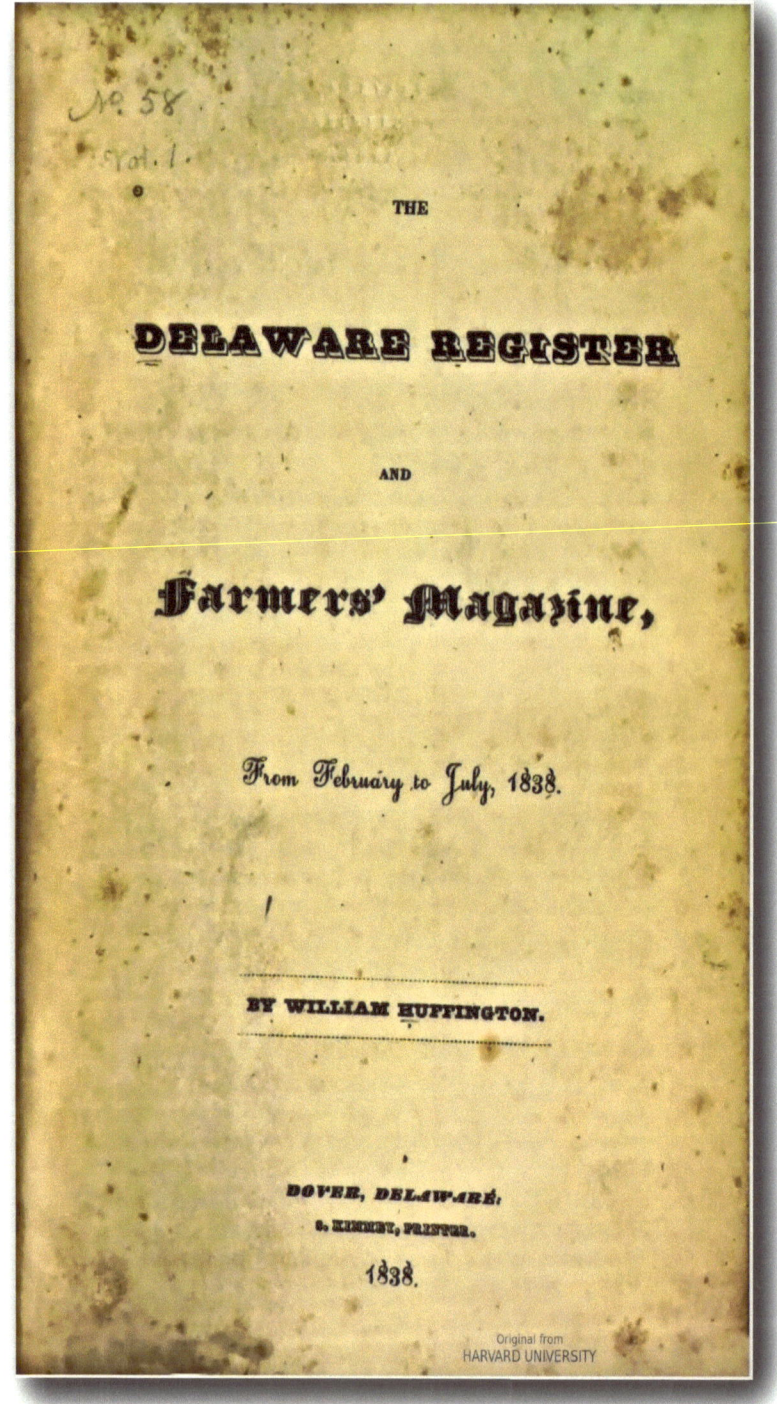

THE

DELAWARE REGISTER

AND

Farmers' Magazine,

From February to July, 1838.

BY WILLIAM HUFFINGTON.

DOVER, DELAWARE:
S. KIMMEY, PRINTER.

1838.

Graffiti

Graffiti, frequently seen as a modern phenomenon, actually has a long international history tracing back to the ruins of ancient Pompeii. Four intriguing stories from Delaware demonstrate this age-old expression of individual identity. (cont. on pg. 84)

Delaware, known as "The First State" & "The Peach State," has pioneering achievements in both American history and agriculture. The fruit's ascension hinged on adoption of novel grafting techniques, attention to soil enhancement, and use of well-defined transport networks. The Delaware peach ruled eastern markets from about 1840 till the turn of the 20th century. (cont. on pg. 85)

The estate of Jehu M. Reed,
"Peach King" of Kent County

Above: The Adjustable Peach Assorter, patented by Mt. Pleasant native John A. Jones in 1874, revolutionized peach sorting by replacing manual labor with a more uniform, efficient, and accurate process. The device's adjustable components facilitated better packing, distribution, and marketability. Its implementation streamlined labor, allowing workers to focus on other tasks and ultimately enhancing productivity, quality control, and supply chain planning.

Right: Delaware Secretary of State John M. Clayton played a pivotal role in advancing railroad technology. Through determined leadership he sought to diminish the state's reliance on waterways. This visionary clearly saw how the iron horse could unlock access to his state's landlocked interior. But competition was afoot. (cont. on pg. 86)

The Moors of Delaware

Warwick Moors Colored School, Millsboro

Delaware's Indian River Inlet offers a fascinating story of mixed-blood families and their origins. Three Moor narratives compete: the *pirate legend* tells of Spanish Moor buccaneers, shipwrecked in the inlet, rescued by Nanticoke Indians. Their community intermarriages led to the mixed-race Delaware Moors. The *colonization legend* has dark-skinned Spanish Moors sailing to America and founding various Atlantic coast settlements. A handful intermarried Indian River Inlet Nanticokes and set up their own cove neighborhoods. The *romantic legend* features Señorita Requa (Miss Reagan), a banished wealthy Spanish woman who relocated onto a plantation near Indian River. One of her slave purchases was in fact a Moorish prince, whom she fell in love with, freed, and wed. Their mixed-heritage children later married into the Nanticoke tribe. Right: Levin Sockum (cont. on pg. 86)

During the 19th century, Mid-Atlantic shipbuilders grappled with the challenge of the narrow Chesapeake & Delaware (C&D) Canal. However, Jonathan M.C. Moore of Bethel devised a working solution. The image above depicts the schooner ram "Edward R. Baird, Jr." Moore designed and launched the craft in Bethel in 1903, sailing it to the Chesapeake Bay via the Nanticoke River. The image is from the collection of the Knowles Museum, Woodland Ferry. Below, a collection of shipbuilder tools on display at the Seaford Museum. (cont. on pg. 87)

In 1842, the Wilmington-based company Betts, Pusey, and Harlan, primarily known for building railroad cars, was a modest operation consisting of just 20 people. However, everything changed dramatically when Samuel Harlan accepted a repair job on the iron cylinder of the wooden steamboat 'Sun' for Captain William Whillidin. This repair job led Betts, Pusey, and Harlan to venture into the shipbuilding industry, resulting in their rapid success. When the Bangor Steam Navigation Company in Maine learned of the shop's repair work and professionalism, they approached Betts, Pusey, and Harlan to construct an iron steamboat from scratch, making them the first iron shipbuilding yard in the USA. (cont. on pg. 87)

VIEW OF THE HARLAN & HOLLINGSWORTH COMPANY'S IRON-SHIP BUILDING ESTABLISHMENT.

The Bangor, built 1843-4

Daniel & Mary Corbit were pillars of the Odessa community. In 1845, the Quaker couple risked it all by harboring a fugitive slave in this tiny attic crawlspace. (cont. on pg. 87)

Delaware Senator John M. Clayton, already a prominent figure, made a savvy 1847 political move by renaming his estate "Buena Vista." This re-branding of his 1845 acquisition served a greater purpose than mere aesthetics. Senator Clayton sought to align himself with Zachary Taylor, a rapidly rising political figure. Taylor had gained fame just months prior as the victorious general in the "Battle of Buena Vista" during the Mexican-American War. (cont. on pg. 88)

Right: The du Pont family amassed generational wealth beginning with gunpowder production. The DuPont mill, located in Brandywine Valley near Wilmington, faced constant explosion threats due to crude processing methods and early safety protections. Accidents were waiting to happen in the combustible plant's working conditions. When stray sparks met gunpowder dust and hell broke loose, family members were left with lasting impressions, unforgettable recollections of horrible blasts, plus tragic loss of life. Despite their immense riches, the du Ponts chose to live near their operations. In 1847, the 45-year-old business was in the midst of supplying gunpowder to the US Government during the Mexican-American War. Ann du Pont recounts how a detonation that year affected her family's home, "Louviers." (cont. on pg. 89)

The farmers who previously worried about locomotives bowling over their cows, the property owners who previously worried about eminent domain overwhelming them—they all reached for their checkbooks. Delaware Railroad stock was hot! In 1836, the Delaware General Assembly chartered the Delaware Railroad with the intention of constructing a line that would span the entire length of the state. This initiative was sparked by concerns that the Maryland Eastern Shore railroad would draw business away from western Delaware towns. However, the Panic of 1837 and the ensuing depression stalled these ambitious plans. In 1849, Samuel M. Harrington, a former Chief Justice of the Delaware Supreme Court, revived the railroad charter. Charles du Pont, a director of the Philadelphia, Wilmington, and Baltimore Railroad, supported Harrington's efforts, urging the people of Kent and Sussex counties to embrace the new transportation development. The revised charter proposed a line from Dona Landing in Kent County to Seaford in Sussex County, with steamships connecting at both ends. This route circumvented towns with vested interests in shipping and shipbuilding industries and eliminated the need to share profits with other railroad lines in New Castle County. (cont. on pg. 89)

Below: Delaware Rail Road Company stock certificate from 1858, signed by Samuel Harrington. **Right:** Track workers used this oil-powered lantern to indicate the end of a control block in Harrington's rail yard. *Both, collection of Harrington Historical Society*

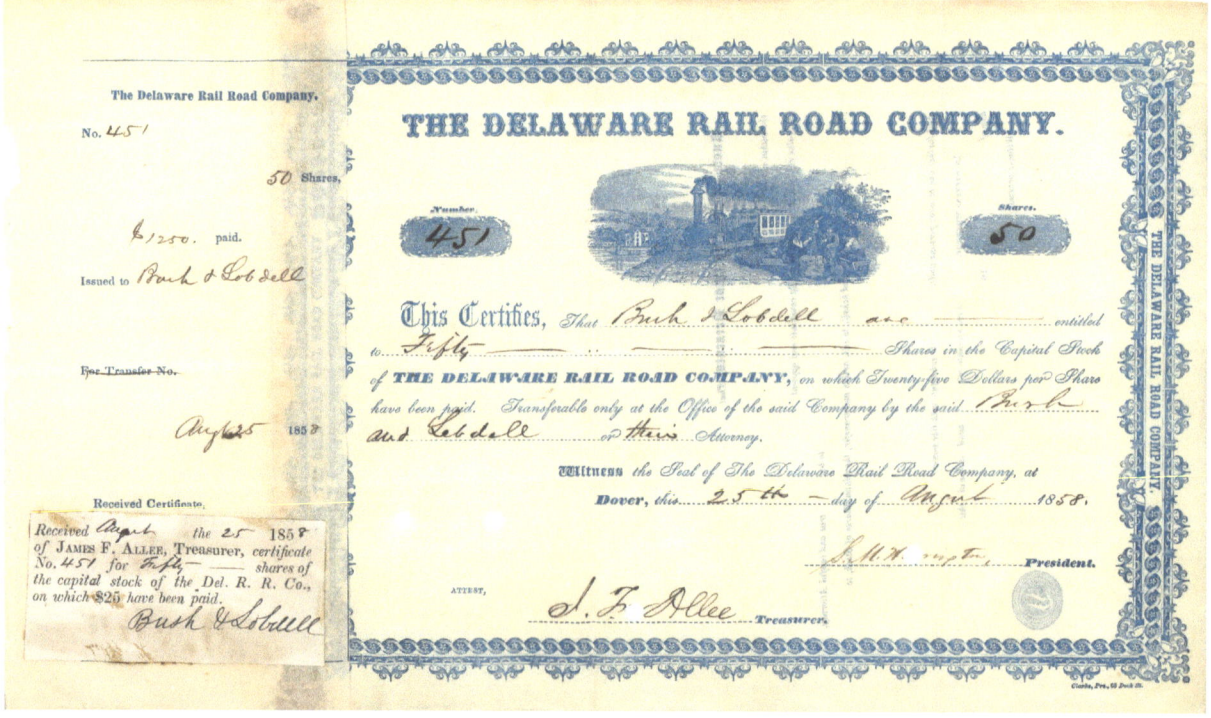

Left: Francis William Edmonds's "The Speculator" (1852). A rural couple listens skeptically to a Building Association representative, identified by the paper in his coat pocket. The salesman—whose top hat, pointed shoes, and umbrella mark him as a city slicker—promises the couple a better life as he unrolls a listing of "1000 Valuable Lots on Rail Road Ave." *Smithsonian American Art Museum, Gift of Ruth C. and Kevin McCann*

Today's Delaware State Fair in Harrington is a delightful mix of cow roping, carnival rides, and cotton candy for casual attendees. However, behind-the-scenes efforts involve hard work. The modern whoopee stands in stark contrast to early, neighborly gatherings. Initially, agricultural fairs played a critical role in boosting the local economy. Exhibitors sought to educate and blue ribbons helped set a standard. (cont. on pg. 89)

Fairview Park. Dover, Del.

It's fitting that the late 19th century doctor's office, preserved today by the Lewes Historical Society, was built and equipped by David Hall (1831-1905). Hall's family was steeped in medical culture and service to the community: Joseph, his grandfather, Henry, his father, and William, his only child, were all physicians. Hall built the structure that housed his practice, as seen here, in the early 1850s. He could be found plying his beloved trade in Lewes for close to half a century at the same location on Savannah Road across from Second Street. Dr. Hall was still in demand even after he sold his building and practice. His dedication was such that he filled his days with house calls, black bag in tow, right up till the time he died. (cont. on pg. 90)

Elizabeth Montgomery (1778-1863), daughter of the renowned Revolutionary War figure Hugh Montgomery, authored numerous vignettes about her hometown in 'Reminiscences of Wilmington' (1851). On the topic of ice skating, she says: "Many can recall hours pleasantly spent at the old barley mill, sliding and skating; groups of young persons and schools assemble here to enjoy the healthy exercise. Those of riper years, too, have had their hours of recreation. In days gone by, A.H. Rowan and two Scotchmen, John Fleming, long a worthy townsman and proprietor of the mill, with his friend William Key, have played a Scotch game called golfing" [she refers to the old Scottish game of curling, not the modern game of golf]. (cont. on pg. 90)

41

Big Thursday

Big Thursday. A day of celebration in the waterman community. The day was also a time for farmers to take a breather: the crops had been planted and were growing nicely; harvest time was still ahead. (cont. on pg. 90)

Opposite page: Early settlers took advantage of the first elevated and dry terrain along the meandering Leipsic River, a location about 5-½ miles upstream from the Delaware Bay. They transformed this buildable portion of the isolated, marshy floodplain into Fast Landing in 1723. The term 'fast' in this context signifies 'firm' or 'secure', indicative of a suitable spot for docking boats. (cont. on pg. 91)

43

BOILING.

GRINDING.

ROLLING.

DIPPING DEPARTMENT.

DRYING.

UNROLLING.

Below: Day in and day out, year after year, the Rehoboth Beach boardwalk magnetically draws seasonal shore vacationers. Visitors have found joy in capturing their seaside memories and sending postcards back home, a time-honored tradition from earliest days.

The Queen Anne's Railroad built their depot to the edge of Rehoboth Beach. A brand new coastal boardwalk simultaneously sprang up in 1884 and instantly attracted shoulder-to-shoulder hordes. (cont. on pg. 91)

Opposite page: This sequence illustration from *Harpers Weekly* highlights the matchmaking process in 1878. America's leading producer of 'kitchen' matches currently manufactures approximately twelve billion 'strikes' per year. The operations of this ultimate matchmaker trace their beginnings to Wilmington. This location provides a clue as to why the company name mimics Delaware's nickname. (cont. on pg. 91)

Left: Take a close look at this log cabin quilt. Its central yellow squares, surrounded by red, indicated a 'safe house.' Underground Railroad conductors used it as a welcome signal. They employed ten quilt patterns in a sequence, guiding runaway slaves. The symbols prepared slaves for escape, later providing directions during their perilous journey. *Note: the Smithsonian Institution asserts this guiding system is just a legend.*

Below: The 1856 'Tilly Escape' through Delaware marked Harriet Tubman's most intricate escape plot to date. The scheme proved her fearlessness to Underground Railroad conductors and station operators. Slaveholders, by contrast, seethed with rage. Photo: Harriet Tubman *(left)*; Tilly *(right)*. (cont. on pg. 92)

Scrapple

This regional breakfast side dish comes to us via Germany's 17th century Palatinate emigrants to Pennsylvania. The name scrapple derives from the curious Middle German phrase "panhas krepel". (cont. on pg. 93)

It's the perfect American Civil War border state story. Look at this 1970 aerial photo of Georgetown's Public Square and Circle. The two circled buildings are the Brick Hotel (bottom) and the site of the Eagle Hotel (right side). One was popular with Confederate sympathizers; one with Union sympathizers. (cont. on pg. 93)

The Civil War cleaved families. It might be easy in today's political climate to dismiss the Delawareans who went south as traitors whose names should be erased from history. But we should remember that the Civil War often presented families with impossible choices. Take the case of Juliette McLane Garesche, a Wilmington native. Her father Louis McLane had served both as a US Senator from Delaware and a US Secretary of State. Her grandfather Allan McLane of Smyrna was a hero of the Revolutionary War. You'd think Juliette would have naturally been a solid supporter of the Union. But she married Peter Bauduy Garesche long before war broke out. They appear to have had a solid marriage, one that produced four children. As the war grew near, Peter's politics veered towards the Confederate cause. Was Juliette expected to leave her husband to remain loyal to the Union? As with many couples of the time, it wasn't a clear choice.

The US Army built Fort Delaware on the tiny, marsh-ridden Pea Patch Island immediately after the War of 1812. The fort's central bay position was perfect for stationing a company charged with safeguarding the upper Delaware Bay. This location also made the fortification a superb site for a prison. Ferry access and fast-moving currents ensured escape from the island was all but impossible. The Union Army chose to re-purpose Fort Delaware as a prison during the Civil War. (cont. on pg. 93)

Opposite: Born in the tumultuous year of 1863 amid the Civil War, astronomer Dr. Annie Jump Cannon went on to make a significant mark on the scientific world. By her passing in 1941, this Dover native had classified more stars by their color spectra than anyone else in the world. Her stellar achievements pioneered a path for future American women astronomers. (cont. on pg. 94)

"During the perilous and unsettled period through which Delaware passed in 1863, there was less disposition to enter the service of the country voluntarily than the preceding year," said historian J. Thomas Scharf. "It soon became evident that a draft would have to be ordered to fill up the quota."

The conscription act that passed in early March immediately brought on howls of protest. For one thing, a draftee could buy his way out for a $300 'commutation' fee. *But.* A blacksmith of that era, one of the better-paid workmen, made about $555 a year. This commutation loophole was for rich men, and the public was furious. (cont. on pg. 94)

Above: The first Delaware Civil War state draft lottery took place in 1863 at The Barracks in Smyrna. The name referred to its supposed use by militia in the War of 1812.

Left: Draft lottery wheel used at the 1863 Smyrna draft board.

Right: Prominent young men from Wilmington formed the Diamond State Baseball Team in 1865. They played their games at the 'playground' on Delaware Ave. and Adams St. The popularity of the 'Rules of 1864' led to the creation of more teams, including the Excelsior Nine and the Quicksteps, by local fans in the city and neighboring towns. In October of that year, the Diamond State Club challenged the Philadelphia Athletics Club to an amateur match. An 1867 tobacco package label depicts an outfielder catching a batted ball 'on the fly'. This all occurred before the era of baseball gloves and the rise of professionalism. *Library of Congress LC-DIG-ppmsca-17526*

The Order of Heptasophs was just one of numerous fraternal secret societies formed after the Civil War. Many later sought to address the nation's enormous need for health and life insurance protections. The Wilmington Conclave met in Red Men's Hall, shown here. (cont. on pg. 95)

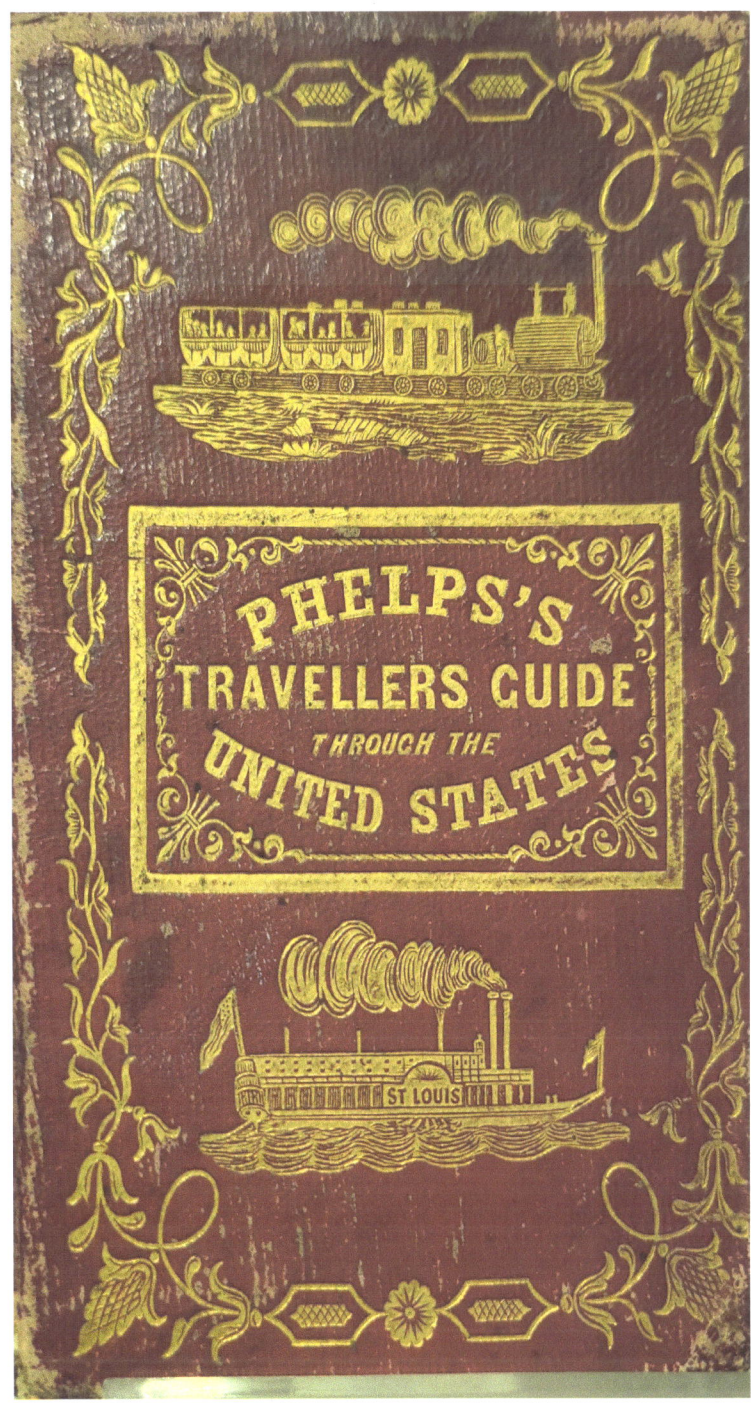

Above: Example of a Morocco Leather book cover. The Morocco Leather industry in Wilmington flourished during the late 19th century, particularly in the classical luxury gloves and handbag markets. The soft, pliable goat skin also found a niche in hardbound bookbinding. The sector's prominence diminished in the 20th century, overcome by the emergence of cheaper alternatives and shifting consumer preferences. (cont. on pg. 96)

Richard Allen, once enslaved in Dover, remembered his former master Stokely Sturgis with affection. Indeed, Sturgis, he said, was "more like a father to his slaves than anything else." Trusting Allen, Sturgis granted him some freedom to work day jobs at a local brickyard or gather firewood to earn spending money. He also permitted Allen and his siblings to partake in local Methodist Society meetings.

Stokely Sturgis was, however, a two-sided coin. Yes, he gave Allen limited freedom but never unfettered freedom without a price. For Sturgis, slavery remained a business. When financial trouble overtook him, the unthinkable cruelty of dividing Allen's family by selling his mother and three of his five siblings overshadowed Sturgis' seeming benevolence. In retrospect, Allen noted "Slavery is a bitter pill," his voice laden with emotion. (cont. on pg. 96)

The African Methodist Episcopal Church built 11 churches in Kent County, between the years 1866 and 1895. Star Hill A.M.E. Church in Dover (right) was the first; St. Paul's in Harrington (above) was the last.

N.B. Smithers

In a well-intentioned prank, Bret Harte and N.B. Smithers tricked their friends. Smithers, a politically connected Latin scholar in Dover, rendered a Latin version of Harte's new poem, "Plain Language from Truthful James," feigning outrage that Harte had plagiarized an ancient piece. His small disclaimer went unnoticed, and the jest escalated into public chaos. (cont. on pg. 97)

Sleighs

Enchanting images of a carefree sleigh ride across the snow-covered countryside to grandmother's house often fail to convey the full picture. Yes, the jingling bells were festive, but they also had a practical role - they served as a signaling device to prevent collisions with other sleighs or pedestrians. (cont. on pg. 97)

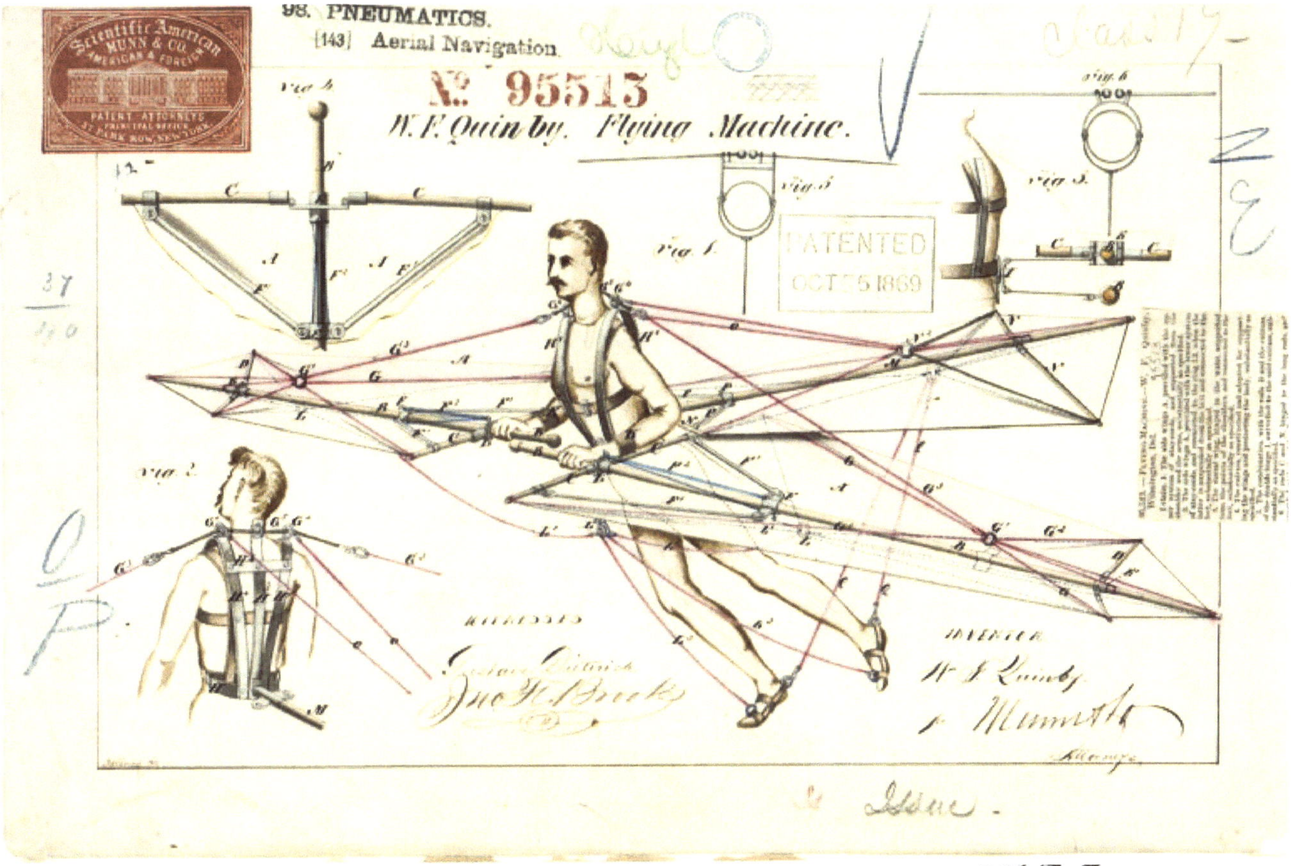

W.F. Quinby (1825-1918) holds a deserving footnote in aviation history. His pioneering role reminds us that the success of the Wright brothers didn't materialize out of thin air; rather, it was partly shaped by the lessons learned from Quinby's failures. (cont. on pg. 98)

Above: The Lewes Station crew had to deal with the winter gale of 1888, one of the most ferocious storms of the 19th century. The station, built by the United States Life-Saving Service in 1884, was the fourth of six stations in Delaware. The post, shown above on a stormy day, was equipped with two Monomoy surfboats, a life-car, a beach cart, and a Lyle gun/breeches buoy rig.

Left: Station crews, known as 'surfmen,' used the breeches buoy as a last ditch effort to rescue mariners when ship decks were too dangerous for surfboats to board. The 1888 storm very nearly killed the Lewes Station surfmen trying to secure a buoy to the shipwrecked schooner *Allie H. Belden*. The horrors they faced that day are almost unimaginable… (cont. on pg 98)

Mihajlo Idvorski Pupin went on to become a world-famous physicist. The Delaware immigrant, at age 16, had just landed his first job in America as a mule driver at a Delaware City farm. Unfortunately, the young Serbian had never taken up check reins to steer a mule team.

(cont. on pg. 99)

Frenchmen invented amalgam fillings, but American dentists were slower to adopt them. Delaware dentist Levin D. Caulk, DDS (1841-1896), true to his surname, emerged as a pioneer in 'caulking' cavities. Caulk mass-produced amalgam and related dental fillings. His products were more cost-effective and safer than earlier fillers like gold and lead. (cont. on pg. 99)

L.D. Caulk's
Camden home, 1877

How about a private duel that takes advantage of disputed state boundaries? One duelist stands on the Maryland side and the other on the Delaware side. Then, any legal challenge ties the competing state court systems in knots. This jurisdictional stalemate appealed mightily to two gentlemen from New York.

(cont. on pg. 99)

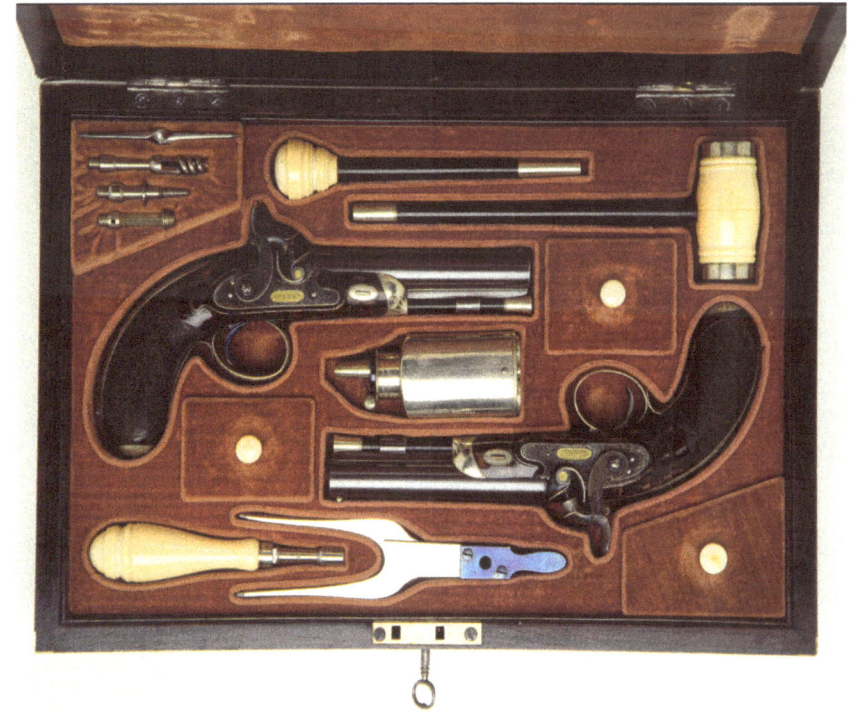

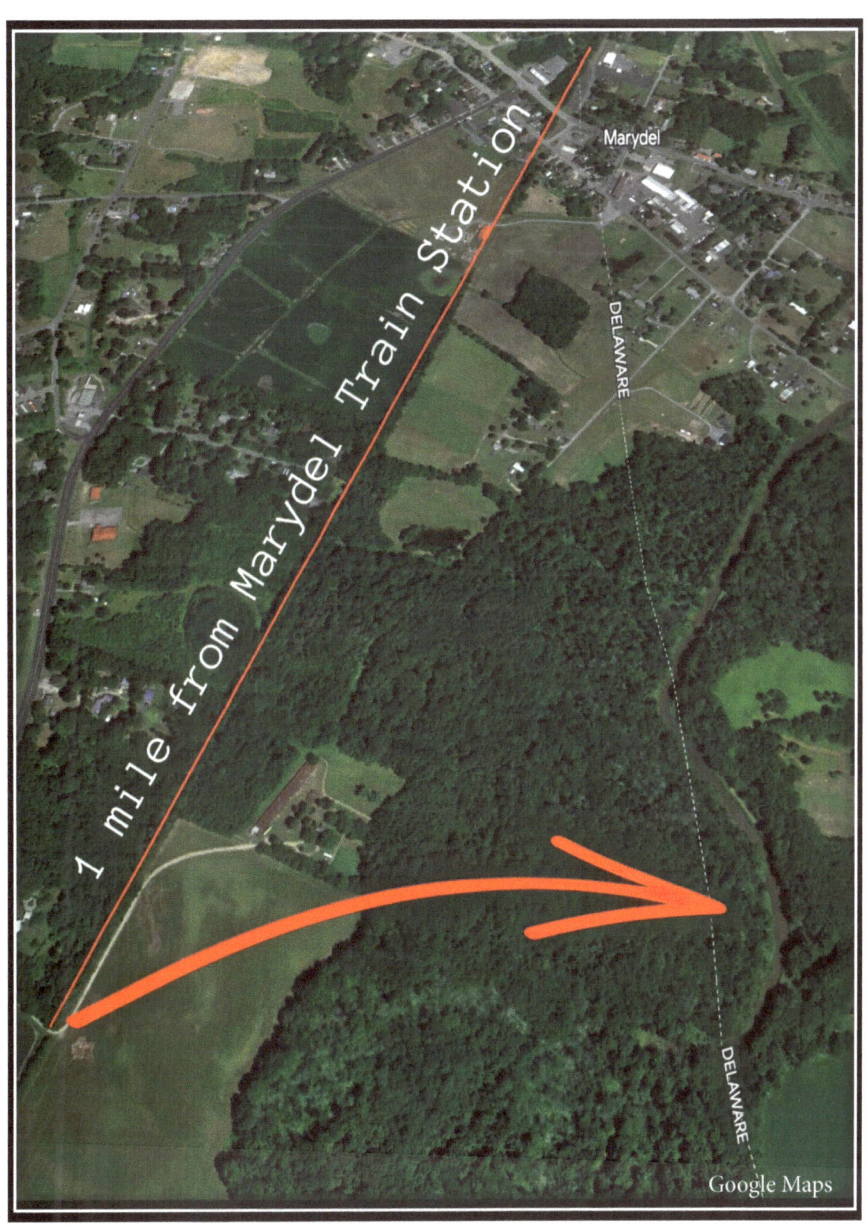

1 mile from Marydel Train Station

Howard Pyle, a pioneering artist from Wilmington, gained fame at the turn of the 20th century for his work as an author and illustrator, notably in books and magazines. He was among the first to illustrate and write a children's story about 'The Merry Adventures of Robin Hood' (1883). An upbeat tone threads throughout 'The Merry Adventures of Robin Hood.' Pyle directly addresses the reader, lacing Robin Hood's exploits with a touch of humor. Below, Pyle's easel set against the backdrop of his Wilmington studio. (cont. on pg. 100)

Suffragist Mabel Vernon (above) worked tirelessly from her position with the Congressional Union for Woman Suffrage to secure passage of the 19th Amendment, giving women the right to vote. A Secret Service agent warned Vernon after forcibly pulled her back from her position just in front of the podium at a 1916 speech President Woodrow Wilson was giving on democracy at the Labor Temple (today's AFL-CIO headquarters) in Washington, DC.

"Mr. President," she called out, "if you consider it necessary to forward the interest of all the people, why do you oppose the national suffrage movement?"

"You mustn't do this again," the agent told her. "I won't, unless it seems necessary," Vernon replied.
(cont. on pg. 100)

History is rife with tales of people faking death to evade debts or romantic woes. If you're going to pull such a ruse, you want people to know about it. Why, then, would anyone believe that writing a sea disaster letter, putting it in a bottle, and casting it into the ocean is a successful strategy? (cont. on pg. 101)

Reverend Tindley preached regularly at Zoar Methodist Church, Odessa, between 1899-1902

Charles A. Tindley's global legacy resonates every time a congregation, choir, or protest group sings "We Shall Overcome". Tindley's uplifting creation stirs the heart, establishing a connection to the divine that shines brightly even today. The work's modern lyrics and tune have evolved over many years. Generations of preachers, choir directors, and protest singers have been inspired to take up and shape Tindley's monumental classic.

Reverend Charles A. Tindley (1851-1933) led a truly extraordinary life straight out of a storybook, building a vast Methodist congregation along the way. He primarily served the African American community up and down the Eastern Seaboard.   (cont. on pg. 102)

The single tax movement built the town of Arden

Left: The movement successfully established an innovative concept of a single land tax in Arden by 1900, yet, this transformation came only after the landed gentry of Dover fiercely resisted the idea four years earlier. Soapbox orators looking for a fair hearing in Dover encountered an unexpectedly harsh response. (cont. on pg. 102)

Opposite: Though it looks like the perfect place for a Hallmark Christmas special, The Green in Dover does have some shadows. The first murder by mail, over a love triangle, for example, took place here. (cont. on pg. 103)

Isaac Jacob Benioff must have felt as though one single day stretched an entire lifetime. A mere moment was etched into his soul forever. He was at his bustling New York City work room when the postal carrier delivered a nondescript package from Viola, DE, a local whistlestop. As he unwrapped what seemed to be just an average box, he was met with a horrific discovery. Inside lay the lifeless body of his baby daughter, a revelation that hit him like a freight train. He hadn't even known that she was gone. Consider the unimaginable shock that any parent would experience. (cont. on pg. 103)

These two essential Victrola components originated from Emile Berliner's earlier designs. Victor Talking Machine Company made crucial engineering adjustments, leading to enhanced music reproduction. As a result Victor's improved products significantly outperformed competitors. (cont. on pg. 104)

The Rural Free Delivery (RFD) system facilitated card and letter communication among family, friends, and acquaintances. RFD ensured access to newspapers and magazines. Customers could now conveniently receive mail-order goods and merchandise. Delaware's RFD journey began in Harrington. (cont. on pg. 105)

Delaware has emerged as the foremost corporate sanctuary due to its conducive legal environment for businesses. More than half of the publicly traded companies on the New York Stock Exchange are incorporated in Delaware. Delaware's lack of physical corporate presence requirements and a low tax structure are particularly advantageous. However, there are other attractive features that distinguish the First State from the rest. Delaware excels in offering a refined, efficient, and reliable legal system and has a more well-defined body of corporate case law to draw on for guidance. Delaware's Court of Chancery system differs significantly from the standard jury trial procedure in other states, eliminating time-consuming courtroom deliberations. The Court of Chancery instead employs judges, known as Chancellors, with deep expertise in business law, leading to quick, informed, and reliable resolutions. While there are five members of the Court of Chancery, each case is heard by a single judge, not a panel. The Court of Chancery judges have established a comprehensive body of guiding decisions. This extensive record provides clarity and predictability to businesses operating under Delaware law and cross references to previous rulings. (cont. on pg. 105)

Tuberculosis in 1905 caused more deaths nationally than typhoid fever and diphtheria combined, claiming 56,770 United States lives. TB caused 150-200 fatalities annually in Wilmington alone. Confusion reigned regarding the causes of "consumption."

Wilmington responded by building its first tubercular (TB) sanitorium in 1907. By year-end, the enterprise was already in deep financial trouble. Emily Bissell's Christmas Seal stamps were a desperate 'Hail Mary pass' to raise additional operational money. (cont. on pg. 106)

Whipping Posts

Sometimes I feel
Sometimes I feel
Like I've been tied
To the whipping post
Tied to the whipping post
Tied to the whipping post
Good lord I feel like I'm dyin'
— **'Whipping Post'**
Allman Brothers Band

Left: An 1868 New Castle whipping attracted a curious crowd; sketched by Earl Shinn for *Harper's Weekly.* **Below:** Dover farmer and folk artist George Kamper carved the life he saw around him. Courtesy Delaware Agricultural Museum. (cont. on pg. 106)

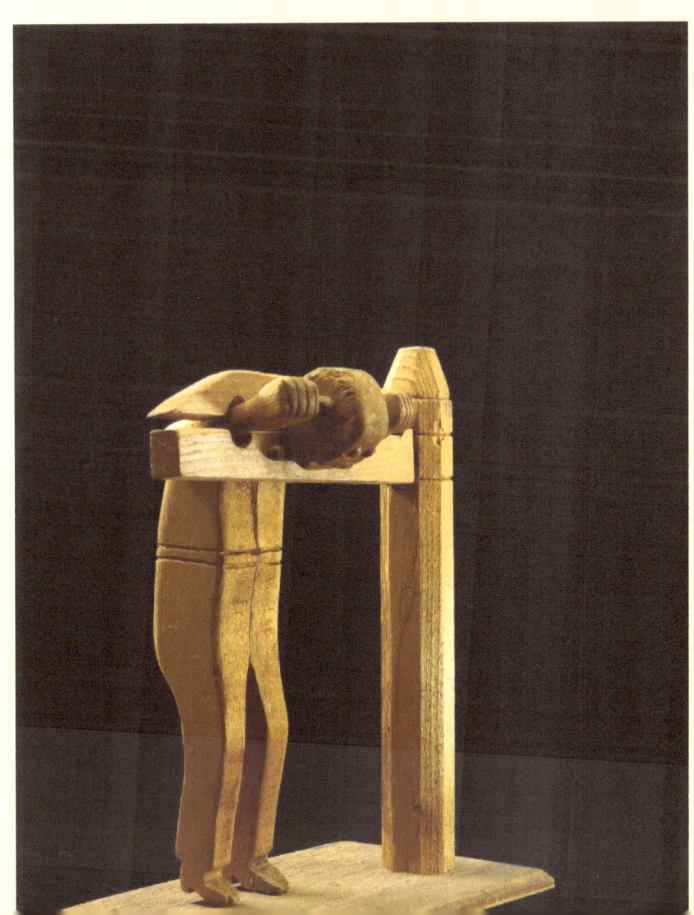

'The Hokey Pokey,' 'The Monster Mash,' and 'Teddy Bears' Picnic' are time-less songs from the American Songbook. These novelty tunes transcend generations. 'The Teddy Bears' Picnic' (1907), an emblem of simpler childhood times, recalls vibrant fantasies and the prominence of playtime. Possibly, the lyrics reflect Tin-Pan Alley composer John W. Bratton's own childhood. Growing up as an only child under his grandmother's care, Bratton probably cultivated a dynamic world of imagination for company. (cont. on pg. 107)

Alfred I. du Pont, American industrialist, financier, and philanthropist, took the helm of Delaware's first horseless carriage. He initially experimented with the steam-driven Stanley Locomobile, Model I, from the Stanley Motor Carriage Company. When he drove the eye catcher through Wilmington in October 1899, the innovative vehicle turned heads and stopped crowds in their tracks. Despite the attention, just two months later du Pont decided to sell the vehicle. At the time of the sale, the car was in good condition and had logged only 400 miles. (cont. on pg. 107)

The horse & buggy could still be seen on roads jostling with the new-fangled automobile for a couple more decades yet. But once the old gray mare was gone, she wasn't replaced. The car was king.

Notes on Photographs

Page 10 Rhoad Built the Roads

Shankland hailed from a well-known Quaker family that had been granted land by William Penn prior to 1700. Perhaps Shankland felt a sense of entitlement, or maybe he considered himself above the law. Whatever the case, his sheer arrogance surfaced when he ran for county sheriff in 1787.

A "Petition from Sussex County to Dover Convention" dated November 28, 1787, is preserved in the archives of the University of Delaware. More than 50 petitioners from Sussex implored state officials to address Shankland's violent tactics, as his armed supporters sought to overthrow the election.

These petitioners "were alarmed on being informed that Rhoad Shankland had declared there were cannon at the [election] place and that … the Coroner of the County [a Shankland accomplice] had said they were determined to carry the Election or lose their lives. These two Gentlemen being seen on the Sunday evening preceding the day going towards the place at the head of a party of men armed with Muskets, your Petitioners were apprehensive they could have no share in the said Election without risquing [sic] the Effusion of Blood."

However, there was no effusion of blood; Shankland was elected. There are no historical records to suggest that he was ever reprimanded for his conduct during the election. In fact, he went on to become a trustee of the county. *Map: Delaware Public Archives; Compass: New Castle Court House Museum*

Page 11 Return Day

Roads are important for trade and communication, especially if voting is in person. However, roads are essential to preserving democracy. Yet in 1787, residents of the western and southwestern portions of Sussex County had to navigate underdeveloped roads. That made travel all the more difficult, in contrast to the more established Delaware counties.

Despite these challenges, voters were expected to make their way to Lewes, the county seat, by horse, buggy, oxcart, or any other means available, to participate in the election. Lewes was predominantly inhabited by liberal Whigs who didn't have far to go, so they naturally turned out in greater numbers. However, conservative Tories from the remote parts of the county complained. Travel difficulties reduced their turnout and thus skewed election results. They also found the effort to close their businesses for two separate days challenging, as they returned home after voting, only to double back to Lewes for the results.

The lingering distrust between Whigs and Tories, which stemmed from the Revolutionary War, concluded just four years prior, made the situation even more volatile. Mobs armed with clubs, muskets, and swords disrupted the election proceedings on three separate occasions, demanding to know the intended votes of citizens. The Delaware Legislature responded by passing a law to move the Sussex polling place to Nanticoke Hundred, near the western end of the state. However, the relocation resulted in a reverse outcome, with only 3% of voters from the coast casting their ballots, while 50% of the voters were local.

The violence and travel issues ultimately led officials to move the Sussex County seat to Georgetown, a more central location not dominated by either party. Polls were open in the 1791 election from Tuesday morning until Wednesday evening, with results announced the following day. The election winners paraded around the town circle in horse-pulled carriages, while the losers and county's political party chairs "buried the hatchet" in a tub of sand. Return Day took place on Thursday, allowing voters to return home after casting their ballots and learning the election results in one trip. *Return Day photo: Delaware Public Archives; early 20th century Return Day carriage: collection Marvel Carriage Museum*

Page 13 Cypress Shingles

The writers of 'Delaware: A Guide to the First State (1938)' marveled that "Some handriven [sic] Pocomoke cypress shingles have worn thin as cardboard after 150 years of weather, but are still as sound as the day they were nailed on hand-hewn oak joists." It stands to reason that a tree that thrives in water is also resistant to rot. However, bald cypress lumber presented challenges, such as splitting, warping, and shrinking if not properly dried before construction. Sussex County loggers faced obstacles in sourcing and transporting bald cypress from difficult-to-access swamps, using specialized equipment to transport the waterlogged wood to building sites.

The use of bald cypress in southern Delaware's colonial architecture reflects the emphasis on practicality, durability, and functionality over ornamental design. The Pocomoke watershed in southern Delaware is the northernmost point where bald cypress grows. The surrounding area was once referred to as the Delaware Everglades, the largest freshwater bog on Delmarva, covering approximately 50 square miles. In 1936, the state drained the swamp by digging a canal, but in 2009, scientists sought to restore the marshland due to its ecological importance. The close-up photo depicts the barn roof at Eden Hill (ca. 1749) in Dover.

Page 12 Conestoga Wagons

During the 18th and early 19th centuries, New Castle gained prominence as a vital port on the Delaware Bay, strategically positioned on the Philadelphia-to-Baltimore route.

Philadelphia and Baltimore, the two cities mentioned, had emerged as dominant industrial centers in the mid-Atlantic region, leading to a need for efficient port-to-port transportation.

Navigating around Delmarva by sea was a time-consuming endeavor. Merchants sought a faster land pathway that would link both the Delaware and Chesapeake Bays. The area's business community determined the path between New Castle and Frenchtown, MD to be most effective. New Castle's port was nearest to Philadelphia and marked the eastern terminus of this crucial connection.

Packet Alley, in New Castle, provided the most direct passage from the docks to the westbound stagecoach and wagon lines. President Andrew Jackson, Davy Crockett, Chief Black Hawk, and many more distinguished figures passed through the shortcut. The alley got its name from packet boats, which started out as mail carriers before they were repurposed for hauling general cargo.

"All vessels bound from Philadelphia to foreign ports stop in New Castle and supply with livestock," stated an 1807 gazette. "A great line of packets and stages passes through from Philadelphia to Baltimore by way of Frenchtown in Maryland. Vast quantities of merchandise are sent to the West. It is at present one of the greatest thoroughfares in the United States. Seven large packet boats sail from New Castle to Philadelphia, ten to fifteen Conestoga wagons cross to Frenchtown, and four large stages [stagecoaches]."

The advent of the railroad, steamboat, and C&D canal by the 1850s diminished the central importance of the New Castle to Frenchtown land route. The old, rutted trail ultimately became just another way to traverse Delmarva. *Conestoga wagon collection Marvel Carriage Museum*

Page 14 Decoy Ducks

Bombay Hook National Wildlife Refuge in central Delaware has always been a major bird migratory stop along the Atlantic coast. This profusion of fowl attracted market and recreational hunters for hundreds of years, with duck harvesting especially lucrative in the early 1800s. Both types of hunters flocked to Delaware from surrounding states, and the canvas-back, the king of ducks, fetched high prices. A savvy gunner could turn a month's work into a year's worth of riches.

Market hunters have been around in Delaware since its earliest years, but the birth of steamboat transport in 1797 revolutionized the industry. Food wholesalers could now ship fresh duck meat to Philadelphia and New York more quickly, leading market hunters to resort to shooting a punt gun and taking down up to 100 birds in one volley to meet the demand. The need for decoys skyrocketed, and market hunters had to attract ever larger flocks of real birds by using 'large spreads of fakes' to stay competitive.

However, the bird population was not sustainable, and in 1839, the Delaware General Assembly banned out-of-state hunters from exporting dead fowl across the state line. Local market hunters started to double down, getting longer punt guns and paying closer attention to the quality of their decoys. This demand for high-quality decoys gave birth to the era of the custom decoy carver.

As the *Middletown Transcript* noted in March 1881, "In the good old times, a gunner could go on the marsh with a half dozen stools [decoys], which might be travesties on the original in both shape and color, and the gunner could lie on a bare ditch bank and kill his 20 ducks a day. Not so now. If a man wishes to make a good day, he must be in a ducking box with twenty or thirty first-rate stools." *Pair of mallard ducks carved by Edgar I. Graef (1914-2005); collection Harrington Historical Society; Canada goose carved by Doug Gibson (1923-); collection Milford Museum; pen & ink shooting scene: collection Hagley Museum & Library*

Page 15 George Washington and the Cherry Tree

What about the story of George Washington chopping down a cherry tree and admitting "I cannot tell a lie"? The legacy of this oft-told tale, and how this yarn was perceived, still resonates. Mason Locke Weems (1759-1825) first published the narrative in his 1800 book, "The Life and Memorable Actions of George Washington".

Weems, also known as Parson Weems, pastored in Anne Arundel County, MD, until 1792. Afterward, he traveled the country selling books door-to-door for Philadelphia publisher Mathew Carey. Weems in 1806 added the "cherry tree fiction" to his book, according to Encyclopedia Britannica.

Weems frequently guest preached while traveling. Reverend James Wiltbank of St. Peter's Episcopal in Lewes observed the parson was widely known for his "noticeable peculiarities. In 1808, Parson Weems was here," Wiltbank writes. "I do not think he was a clergyman, notwithstanding his story about the Bishop of London having ordained him. If he had been ordained, he could have shown his credentials, his Letters of Orders from the Bishop of London. He certainly was very clever." "Encyclopedia Britannica" confirms Weems was, in fact, ordained in the Anglican church in London in 1784.

Reverend Wiltbank goes on to say, "His 'Life of George Washington' was a household work for many years. It is the only source for the famous story of 'the hatchet and the cherry tree.' The incidents Weems records of Washington's youth have in them nothing that is marvelous or even uncommon. They are ordinary events that occur in the life of many well-raised boys. And yet, because Weems has been discredited by some writers, and because these incidents have no other recorder than Weems, they have been ridiculed and denied by even historical writers."

How did Parson Weems's charming story manage to survive to this day, despite the scorn heaped on him by skeptical contemporaries? The answer is attributable to publisher William Holmes McGuffey, who included the "cherry tree and the hatchet" tale in his widely circulated grammar school textbook, "The McGuffey Reader," which endured from 1836 until the early 20th century.

Page 17 Covered Bridges

The Wooddale Bridge in Wilmington, built in 1860, employs a "Town lattice truss" for structural support. This design was patented in 1829 by Ithiel Town, a nationally renowned architect. The truss construction, known for resilience against severe storms, uses wooden pegs, or "trunnels," instead of nails to hold the bridge's frame together. In 1982, the Delaware Department of Transportation (DelDOT) reinforced the bridge by adding steel I-beams beneath the deck, to enhance its strength and durability.

Ashland Bridge's builders also used Ithiel Town's lattice truss design, erecting a structure almost identical to the nearby Wooddale Bridge. Ashland Bridge (1860), also known as the Barley Mill Road Covered Bridge, spans New Castle County's Red Clay Creek on a hairpin turn at the bottom of the steep Red Clay Valley. The Wilmington and Western Railroad struggled to blast an 1871 cut through an adjacent rock ridge. This opening was so narrow that fast trains risked scraping against the excavated sides. The W&WR built a depot in the area, and a US Postal Service pickup station followed in 1873. This section of Wilmington was a bucolic area in the late 19th century, where nearby picnickers would often spread blankets.

The currently used Smith's Bridge is the fifth bridge built on this site, the original dating to 1816. All five spans were named after Isaac Smith, who with his partner Joseph Brinton, operated a flour mill in Beaver Valley, along Brandywine Creek. The first covered bridge was swept away in an 1822 flood, rebuilt, and in 1828 suffered the same fate. The 1839 version remained standing until 1954, when it was scheduled for demolition. State Engineer William McWilliams successfully petitioned DelDOT to save the bridge as one of the state's last remaining covered bridges. DelDOT then reinforced the structure with a steel deck supported by stone piers. Arsonists partially burned the bridge in 1961. State crews repaired and reopened Smith's Bridge, minus the covering, to traffic in June the following year. DelDOT finally covered the bridge in 2002 and updated the restoration with a Burr Arch Truss made of Bongossi wood, an African hardwood renowned for its natural resistance to decay, rot, and fire. Governor Ruth Ann Minner dedicated the refurbished Smith Bridge on January 11, 2003.

Page 18 Fleatown

Travelers were surely relieved to come upon Samuel Warren's tavern/inn on one side of the Fleatown clearing and Milleway White's watering hole on the other. In those days, this area was the backcountry, the wilderness, the frontier. Lodgings, as a result, were few and far between. Both White and Warren offered barebones accommodations.

Fleatown's quirks might have surprised travelers accustomed to a more sophisticated style of innkeeping. The tale of the goose who tended bar illustrates the point. A young lawyer named John M. Clayton frequently traveled this route in the 1820s. Years later he fondly remembered how one day he entered Warren's establishment. The proprietor was absent, but a large gray gander was strolling up and down in front of the bar. The bird let out three loud screeches, and the proprietor, working his field, came running to serve Clayton a drink.

Stagecoach passengers were the only non-agricultural source of business in this tiny crossroads, so White and Warren competed fiercely for their trade. According to *The Morning News* [Wilmington], both establishments offered "the cleanest of beds and a bill of fare that would tempt the appetite of the most fastidious epicurean." Warren's inn was especially famous for its late-night revelries. When asked to describe them in 1895, retired Superior Court Judge Charles M. Cullen would only say "peaches and honey" with a twinkle in his eye.

Milleway White passed away in 1832, and Samuel Warren promptly bought and shut down his establishment. During this period, the town struggled to lure new businesses and residents. To rejuvenate the area, locals renamed the crossroads Federalsburg. Despite this strategic rebranding, the community's fate remained unchanged. With the emergence of the railroad, which replaced stagecoaches as the primary travel method, Federalsburg started to steadily decline. After Warren's death in 1843, his business found no buyers. As railroads spread and transformed landscapes everywhere, they foreshadowed imminent changes. The Delaware Railroad built the Ellendale station only two miles away from Federalsburg, effectively sealing the little burg's fate. *Stagecoach photo: collection Smithsonian Institution*

Page 19 Solomon Bayley

"I sat there and looked right at them," he wrote later in an autobiography about his dangerous journey to freedom, "and thought I, … here they come's right toward me … Am I going to sit here until they come and lay hands on me?"

The remains of a large fallen tree, now an elongated stump, offered a temporary hiding place for the terrorized fugitive. He threw himself face down, peeking only long enough to see one of the slave hunters waving a forked stick back and forth. A conjurer's rod, perhaps? The other looming stalker carried a large club. He veered off to one side, clueless. The first man stopped suddenly. He seemed to have picked up the trail. Then: "He h'ant gone this way." The conjurer swung the wand in a different direction. "Come, let us go this way." His wrong turn created the pivotal moment.

Solomon had seen the whites of their eyes while his heart raced. Then he remembered seeing a flock of birds circling around him at dusk as he lay down to sleep. Surely this halo had been a sign from God he would be protected. Solomon breathed free at last, and the words "Stand still and see the salvation of the Lord" rang through his mind. They had not cornered him!

Now the threat had passed, and Solomon continued crouching, and prayed what to do next.
The well-placed stump, and Solomon Bayley's (1771-1839) steadfast faith, let him live for another day. Now he could navigate his way to freedom, heading north after a harrowing crisis.

This 1799 close call drove Solomon to keep going straight to his native Kent County, knowing the town of Camden to be a runaway slave safe haven. Quakers, their abolitionist views newly forming, had set up the Camden Congregation of Friends in 1788. Solomon was no doubt familiar with the Quaker Meeting Society and their activities on behalf of the black community. Many years later, Solomon wrote a widely read autobiography, "A Narrative of Some Remarkable Incidents..." (1825), in which he detailed his bolt for freedom—planting the idea for Camden as a future stop on Delmarva's Underground Railroad.

Twelve years after Solomon Bayley's death, the future famed Underground Railroad conductor Harriet Tubman (1820-1913) made her own escape from slavery. She was born in Dorchester County, MD, about 75 miles from Camden. Plantation owners actively suppressed slaves from learning news of the outside world. In an 1897 interview, Tubman cited William and Nat Brinkley, along with Abraham Gibbs, as her Camden Underground Railroad conductors.

It is entirely possible that Tubman was not aware of Camden as a safe stop for escaping slaves until she encountered Philadelphia abolitionist William Still and others in his circle. They, in turn, were familiar with Bayley's autobiography and used his path-blazing saga to help Tubman map her specific Delmarva Underground Railroad escape routes. Thus, Kent County native Solomon Bayley helped pave the way for Harriet Tubman's Delaware success.

Page 20 Bog Iron Industry

Colonel William D. Waples established the Millsborough Charcoal Furnace on the Indian River, a tributary of the Nanticoke, about 8 miles south of Georgetown in 1815. Named after the dome-roofed blast furnace used in the foundry, the furnace stood in what is now known as Cupola Park. Waples used local bog iron as raw ore to produce pig iron and cast iron.

Bog iron forms from the anaerobic oxidation of iron in boggy or swampy areas and is a naturally occurring iron ore. This renewable iron source allows for continuous extraction. The smelting process, where iron ore combines with carbon, results in pig iron, a rudimentary form of iron. High carbon content makes pig iron brittle and unsuitable for direct use. Cast iron, with a high carbon concentration, exhibits excellent fluidity when molten, making it ideal for molding into intricate shapes, such as pipes and cookware. Pig iron is primarily used as a raw material for the production of steel and other iron-based alloys in the manufacturing industry.

A shrewd businessman, Colonel Waples also owned several other enterprises, including a stagecoach line that traversed the peninsula with Millsboro as a crucial stop.

Samuel G. Wright, a New Jersey entrepreneur, bought a small interest in the Millsborough Charcoal Furnace in 1822. As a result, the newly recapitalized organization added a foundry to its operations. Six years later, Colonel Gardiner H. Wright, Samuel Wright's son, joined the business.

The combined ventures produced 450 tons of industrial pig iron and 350 tons of casting annually by 1830. The forge's output increased to 600 total tons of pig iron and castings per year within three years. To produce this output, the Millsborough Charcoal Furnace consumed 180,000 bushels of charcoal fuel annually. Forgemasters used 7,000 bushels of oyster shells per year as a flux to remove iron ore impurities. *The Daily Times* [Salisbury, MD] reported that the company employed 80 men who worked 12-hour days at $18 per month.

Delmarva News noted that, at the industry's height, wagons stood head to tail waiting to be unloaded with bog iron from the furnace, out past Five Forks toward Hickory Hill. The Millsborough Charcoal Furnace shipped products to places like Boston, New York, Philadelphia, Baltimore, and Norfolk in the early 1830s. Better grades of ore were available to furnaces elsewhere in America, forcing Gardiner Wright to shut down the furnace in 1836.

Despite the closure of the furnace, the company's foundry division continued, producing pipes for the Croton Water Works in New York in 1837. It also manufactured the railings surrounding Independence Square in Philadelphia and the city's Eastern Penitentiary castings. Gardiner Wright, now the sole owner of the Millsborough Charcoal Furnace, operated the only remaining Delaware furnace/foundry by 1859. Although the business persisted until 1879, the commercial iron industrial phase of Sussex County's history was destined to end due to the local ore's poor quality. *Photos: 48" iron pipes at NYC's 135th St Gatehouse / NYC Municipal Archives Digital Collections dep88-40ls65w; State House and Independence Square, 1868. Albumen Prints. Free Library of Philadelphia: Philadelphia, PA.*

Page 21 Communion Tokens

The practice of using communion tokens in Presbyterian churches varied. Generally, once a congregant had been admitted to communion and received a token, they were not required to undergo retesting before each communion service.

In some churches, new tokens were issued annually, potentially requiring a repeated examination. In others, the same token could be used for several years. These practices were influenced by local customs and ministerial preferences.

Presbyterian communion tokens were typically made of inexpensive and durable materials. The most common material was metal, particularly lead, pewter, or copper, but tokens could also be made of other materials such as wood or bone. The choice of material often depended on what was readily available and affordable. For instance, starting in the 1700s, worshipers at Lewes Presbyterian Church used copper communion coins.

Tokens could be marked with the church or minister's initials and occasionally a date. During worship services, congregants would deposit their tokens into a wooden box akin to a collection plate.

The system was susceptible to misuse. Wayward church members could obtain tokens through illicit means. Furthermore, church elders, often wielding considerable power, could withhold tokens from individuals undergoing church discipline, whether justly or unjustly.

Around 1825, the use of communion tokens began to phase out as churches transitioned towards more inclusive practices. By the mid-19th century, the custom had largely ceased. *Token photograph collection Presbyterian Historical Society*

Page 22 Patty Cannon

The life of Patty Cannon would make for a compelling silver-screen narrative. This notorious slave bounty hunter's ruthless reputation reverberated across the Maryland and Delaware borders.

The infamous Cannon, at the helm of her criminal enterprise, capitalized on the anxieties and injustices of her era. Her gang hunted down those who had escaped bondage in Maryland, as well as free African Americans residing in southern Delaware, only to sell them back into Maryland slave traders' clutches. This grim reality of slave bounty hunting underscores a disturbing chapter in America's era of slavery.

Authorities in southern Delaware began scrutinizing her activities. Cannon felt compelled to broaden her operations into less conspicuous territories. This strategic shift led her to the streets of distant Philadelphia, where she abducted black children, only to traffic them to slave traders even further away in Mississippi.

The law finally caught up with Cannon's nefarious doings in April 1829. Officials unearthed the bodies of several murder victims, including a young child and infant. While most of Cannon's gang managed to evade capture, the slave bounty hunter herself was apprehended and imprisoned in Sussex County jail.

Cannon's story reached its dark conclusion a month later. She died in her cell, still awaiting trial for murder. The circumstances surrounding her death are shrouded in controversy and legend.

"She obtained some poison and poisoned herself," according to E.E. Barclay in Narrative and confessions of Lucretia P. Cannon.

Local legend weaves a tale of a henchman ingeniously using the courthouse's newel post as a secret compartment to hide a vial of retrievable arsenic for Patty. Historians have met this narrative with skepticism.

"[Cannon] expressed a desire to be visited by a priest," explains Barclay, "in order that she might make a confession of the dreadful crimes she had committed. Accordingly, one was sent for, and she made her confession nearly as follows:

" '*She said that she had killed eleven persons with her own hands and had also been accessory to the murder of more than a dozen others, and that she herself killed the traveler, last mentioned, and that she had been guilty of the shocking crime of murdering one of her own offspring, by strangling it when three days old, and that she also poisoned her husband, and that she and one of her gang had just laid their plans for murdering in their beds two of her neighbors who were considered wealthy, and that they should have committed the murders if they had not been arrested.' "*

The original courthouse where Cannon was to be tried is no longer standing, and the modern one has been extensively renovated.

Patty Cannon's legacy serves as a chilling reminder of the ruthless exploitation and brutal experience of both enslaved and free African-Americans. Her story also underscores the enduring necessity for vigilance and justice in confronting human trafficking and the violation of human rights in every age.

Page 23 Cannon's Ferry

Jacob Cannon's episode stirred the curiosity of Delaware writer George Alfred Townsend. He captured the yarn in his novel "The Entailed Hat" (1884), and it remains the only published documentation of the story. Otherwise, his saga of Jacob Cannon's life matched newspaper articles, genealogical records, and historical journals of the day (1820s-1840s). *Ferry drawing: Delaware Historical Society; Cannon House: Delaware Public Archives*

Page 24 Delaware Breakwater

Concerned by the increasing number of shipwrecks, Congress deliberated over potential solutions. In 1827, Senator Levi Woodbury of New Hampshire, who served as the Chairman of the Senate Commerce Committee, led the proposal to construct a protective breakwater off the coast of Lewes. Woodbury and his fellow senators contended that Delaware, New Jersey, and Pennsylvania could not individually shoulder the expense. They maintained that the resulting boost in regional commerce from the new shelter would benefit a broader area, thus justifying the nation's investment.

Not all Americans supported the plan to construct a breakwater off the coast of Delaware. Natchez, MS citizens, for example, demanded their share, with *The Statesman & Journal* arguing that the Mississippi River system, which had 130 steamboats navigating its waters, deserved equal government consideration. South Carolina and Missouri delegations shared these concerns. President Andrew Jackson and his supporters generally advocated for a laissez-faire economic approach, opposing the Whig modernization and growth agenda. Consequently, Jacksonian Democrats voted against the breakwater appropriations bill.

Despite the opposition, the Whigs held the majority, and on May 23, 1828, Congress allocated $250,000 for Lewes' new mile-long breakwater to be constructed in a 'rubble mound' style. The breakwater, made from rocks piled on the seabed, would have a wide base that narrowed towards the top. A protective layer of large rocks would cover the mound to prevent erosion. The construction process involved quarrying and transporting rocks, then placing them on the seabed using derricks. New Castle County's Bellevue Quarry was contracted by the US Treasury to provide the stone. Starting in late 1829, the quarry supplied approximately 130,000 tons of Brandywine granite, or "blue rock," annually for the six-year construction. Wagons transported the stone blocks to Wilmington's docks, where barges carried them to the Delaware Bay.

Stone setters at the breakwater site did not require diving bells, as the shallow 24-36 feet low-tide water depth in Lewes Harbor allowed barge-based crews to use derrick winches. Completed in 1835, the Delaware Breakwater became the Western Hemisphere's first such structure. Between 1839 and 1843, an average of 22 ocean-going vessels sought refuge behind the bay's southern barrier annually. The breakwater fulfilled its purpose, but the final cost exceeded eight times the initial budget.

Meanwhile, continuing tensions between states' rights and federal control persisted. In 1850, President Millard Fillmore, a New Yorker, reassured southern constituents in his annual message to Congress, stating that prudent public works expenditures were not solely for local benefit. He emphasized that the Delaware Breakwater supported not only the states around the bay and river but also the entire nation's coastal navigation and, to a significant extent, foreign commerce. This north-south disagreement smoldered right up to 1861, the beginning of the Civil War. *Quarry excavation photo: collection Lewes History Museum; Breakwater postcard: Delaware Public Archives*

Page 25 New Castle and Frenchtown Rail Road

Two issues arise when a horse works on a rail structure atop wooden crossties: 1) the horse, forced to step over ties, slows down and tires quickly, and 2) the horse's shoes inevitably damage the timbers, hastening deterioration and escalating maintenance costs. The solution? Mount the rails on stone blocks, leaving an unobstructed path between them. Thus, the railroad's initial 9 miles employed granite "sleepers" rather than wooden crossties, embedded in a ballast bed for stability.

"The manner of building a railway," noted the *Charleston* [SC] *Daily Courier*'s editor on April 30, 1825, "may be learned from how the dam-way between Bennet's two water saw-mills was constructed years ago, using posts, sleepers, and braces. This framework can be wood, stone, or iron. To make it a railway, rails are placed on the sleepers, fitting the carriage wheel and setting it on top."

What transpired in the remaining 7-1/2 miles after the initial 9 miles? Technology was advancing. Expenses skyrocketed, with stone block-supported railways costing nearly $6,000 per mile, as writer Nicholas Wood detailed in 'A practical treatise on rail-roads' (1830). He added that wooden sleepers were more cost-effective. However, the more significant transformation was the emergence of steam locomotives. Considered experimental in 1809, by 1827, they captivated the British public. In 1829, George Stephenson conclusively demonstrated the steam locomotive's superiority over horses with his engine, "The Rocket," which pulled two coaches compared to a horse's one. Soon, he secured a contract for the first inter-city passenger railway between Liverpool and Manchester.

NC&F's proprietors took note. In 1831, before their line's inauguration, they approached Robert Stephenson, George's son, about acquiring an innovative engine. The completed NC&F line opened on February 28, 1832, initially using horses to pull a single coach along cast, and later wrought iron, rails. By September, a new steam locomotive arrived from Britain, marking the end of Delaware's early horse-drawn railway era.

Page 26 Wilmington Whaling

WWC's second ship, the *Lucy Ann*, joined the fleet in July 1835, setting sail in September under the command of Captain J. J. Parker and officers from New Bedford, MA. Following closely, the *Superior* departed in December 1835 with Captain Heman Crocker at the helm.

By March 1836 the *Lucy Ann* had gathered a significant amount of whale products. The company's fourth ship, *North America*, made its way from New York in June of the same year.

This fleet buildup signaled a growing new chapter in the company's operations. Because of this, WWC managed to secure a $15,000 government appropriation in 1836 to upgrade Wilmington's harbor.

The *Lucy Ann* returned to Wilmington in April 1837, laden with a $26,000 bounty consisting of 4,400 barrels of whale oil, 300 barrels of sperm oil, and 11,000 lbs. (about twice the weight of an elephant) of bone. Such was the ship's weight that parts of its cargo had to be unloaded before it could dock at the Wilmington wharves.

The *Superior* stockpiled 1,200 barrels of oil in February 1838 and prepared for a Japanese coastal journey. Come June 1839, WWC purchased the *Jefferson*, its fifth ship, in Baltimore. "Really, our neighbors in Wilmington are driving a 'whaling' business," the *Baltimore Sun* commented with a chuckle.

A March 1841 hurricane destroyed the *North America* in Geography Bay, New Holland (modern-day Australia). WWC reeled from the impact. They sought to gloss over losses by offering investors a seven percent stock dividend in August 1841. The ploy only resulted in market over-optimism. The company struggled from that point on. Multiple unsuccessful trips dealt a never-ending blow of diminishing profits.

In June 1845, in a decision that signaled the end of an era, the Wilmington Whaling Company was compelled to halt all future operations. Its maritime ambitions had been stunted significantly, having managed to launch just five of an intended ten ships, with one tragically lost at sea.

The entire industry was caught in a swift and unyielding downswing. The advent of cheaper and safer lighting alternatives, such as coal oil and kerosene, accelerated this decline. Almost overnight, their practicality and affordability rendered the traditional whaling industry obsolete. *Pages 138 & 288 from the logbook of Wilmington Whaling Company ship* Lucy Ann, *on its November 28, 1841 to June 14, 1844 voyage. Henry King, master. John F. Martin, keeper and illustrator. Both images courtesy of the New Bedford Whaling Museum / NBWM Research Library, KWM 434.*

Page 27 Newark College formed

The Presbytery of Lewes petitioned the Philadelphia Synod in 1741, highlighting the necessity for clergy educated in the middle colonies. Francis Alison answered the call and established a free school in New London, PA, providing instruction in languages and other subjects.

"This Free-School opened at the House of Mr. Alison in Chester County for the Promotion of Learning where all Persons may be instructed in the Languages and some other Parts of Literature, without any Expenses for Their Education," noted the *Pennsylvania Gazette* on November 24, 1743.

Alison left his New London Academy in 1752, moving to Philadelphia to run a grammar school at Benjamin Franklin's request. He later returned to Newark in 1767 with some of his pupils to run the Newark Academy.

The Synod chose Newark for its strategic location, close to Philadelphia, Delmarva, and the southern colonies. The town was described as "a suitable and healthy village, not too rich or luxurious, where real learning might be obtained."

Alison was a leading scholar in America during his time. Four of his students became members of the Continental Congress who signed the Declaration of Independence (Thomas McKean and George Read, signing for Delaware, and Dr. Benjamin Rush and James Smith, signing for Pennsylvania.)

Francis Alison's academy ultimately led to the University of Delaware, though his dream of transforming his academy into a full-fledged college wasn't realized till the Newark Academy's trustees secured a charter for New Ark College.

The new college aimed to educate students in languages, mathematics, and natural philosophy. Architect Winslow Lewis designed the college's Greek Revival style building based on earlier plans by US Capitol architect William Strickland. He began construction on the 6-acre tract in late 1832.

"Manlove Hayes, a Dover boy who later became a trustee of the college but was then a student at the academy," Delaware historian John A. Munroe tells us, "was playing with other boys around the open trenches prepared for the college foundation and asking questions of the man in charge of the masonry when the latter handed him a brick and showed him how to place it in the corner of the trenches, telling him he could ever after remember that he laid the first brick." The new building was ready for occupancy by May 1834.

The University of Delaware, a public land-grant research institution, now anchors Newark. Its seal bears the date 1743, reflecting the founding of the New London free school. Francis Alison's accomplishments stand as testament to his significant contributions to the educational landscape of America and the Presbyterian Church. *Photo collection of Delaware Historical Society*

Page 28 First Magazine in the State

Before his publishing career, William Huffington (1793-1861) practiced law in Dover for 15 years. At that point, he became more interested in politics and literature than his chosen profession. Despite his lack of prior publishing experience, his magazine gained immediate attention for its emphasis on history, interviews with notable figures, and practical advice. *The Native American*, a Washington, DC-based newspaper, praised the publication for effectively capturing the "national taste." The paper went on to emphasize the importance of Delawareans placing their history within the context of America's overall identity.

The Delaware Register lacked advertisements, relying solely on subscriptions for funding. It was published in a perfect-bound, 6x9 format with substantial page counts, designed to be kept on bookshelves rather than casually read and discarded. Huffington's goals for the publication included: a) providing a comprehensive history of Delaware; b) educating local farmers on progressive agricultural techniques; and c) featuring accounts of public institutions, human interest stories, and travelogues. While he included poetry and welcomed reader contributions, Huffington avoided incendiary topics such as sex, politics, and religion.

The magazine never took off as expected. According to historian J. Thomas Scharf, "This periodical, though well edited, was discontinued at the close of one year, the enterprise being too far ahead of its time."

Despite its short run, *The Delaware Register and Farmer's Magazine* remains a historical example of early publishing in Delaware.

Page 29 Graffiti

First, in the top left photo, the name "A. Finney" is meticulously etched into the side of the Hale-Byrnes House in Stanton. David Finney owned this northern Delaware house for 20 years. The true identity of the person who carved the name remains a mystery. Finney's wife and daughter were both 'Ann.' So which "A. Finney" carved her initials?

The top right photo showcases a gristmill carving from the town of Marydel. Various names have been associated with the mill, built in 1756 by David Marsdin. The Medford family owned this mill, situated where the Choptank River meets Mud Mill Pond, from 1898-1987. As a result, the original graffiti likely read 'Medford.' Observe the wooden beam at the top of the photo and the concrete support interface. The concrete's texture differs at this juncture, suggesting that the 'Me' portion of the scrawl has been obscured.

In the bottom right photo, the "EJ" initials carved into the back of a pew at the Camden Friends Meeting House likely resulted from mischievous intentions. Church records identify the culprit as young Eskill Jenkins (1822-1873). We know the scalawag grew up in the congregation and is buried in the adjacent cemetery.

Lastly, in 1838, the enigmatic "HB" carved initials into the door of the Old Swedes Church in Wilmington. Why did HB do it? Like so many, the identity and motives of this individual remain unknown.

These lesser-known, personal anecdotes of yesteryear remind us that history encompasses more than just dry dates and faded documents. The people of Delaware's past shared many of our quirks and imperfections. The ancestral stories told around these antiquated markings help to humanize them.

Page 30 Delaware Peach Industry

Isaac Reeves played a pioneering role in Delaware's peach industry. He promoted the innovative "budded tree" grafting technique in his Delaware City orchards. Although the state had other peach growers, Reeves' method of grafting scions from the best-producing trees yielded superior fruit.

Philip Reybold, one of his neighbors, was an enterprising individual willing to explore any opportunity. Recognizing the commercial potential of Reeves' propagation technique, Reybold combined it with a seemingly unrelated opportunity, giving rise to a lucrative new venture.

The Chesapeake and Delaware Canal Company, in the 1820s, contracted with Reybold and his crew to excavate the Delaware City to St. Georges portion of the canal. The digging required the removal of large amounts of earthen material that included a mixture of clay, sand, rock… and marl.

"Reybold was what we would call a smart cookie," observed *News Journal* [Wilmington] columnist Bill Frank in a 1984 article. "He hired workers to dig the canal, then took over the contract to feed them. When he saw the soil being dug up, he learned that it was known as marl because it contained remains of prehistoric sea shells, valuable as fertilizer. He sold this soil to neighboring farmers and used it on his own farm."

Like many other orchardists in his time, Reybold lacked formal training in agriculture and instead gained practical knowledge through hands-on experience. Fascinated by the positive use of marl, he discovered through trial and error that it greatly enhanced peach cultivation. Reybold became a passionate advocate for soil amendment and encouraged his neighbors to adopt the practice.

He and his five sons managed a 117,000 peach tree empire by 1842. They shipped their fruit to wholesale fresh markets in Philadelphia and New York on their own steamships in a steady parade. The family's success played a significant role in the growth of New Castle County's peach industry.

Jehu Reed, a prominent Kent County competitor, posed a significant challenge to Reybold's expanding enterprise. Prior to the advent of steam, Reed whisked his initial peach harvests in fast sailing vessels from Bower's Beach to Philadelphia. The sizable gold payments from urban markets astounded many Murderkill Hundred residents. The upshot? Reed's pioneering efforts in out-of-state marketing led to a stampede of widespread Kent County peach cultivation. From 1829 to 1868, Reed also invested in a substantial fruit tree nursery, introducing ten peach varieties, including Lemon Cling, Morris White, and Early York Opening.

Reed and Reybold shared a mutual appreciation for the importance of soil management in their commercial operations. Reed used ground horseshoe crab shells, also known as "king crab" shells, as a natural soil additive. He established a processing plant at Warren's Landing to supply ground shells for himself and his neighbors. Furthermore, Reed passionately supported agricultural education and worked tirelessly to teach the local community how to effectively restore the county's fields.

In the 1890s, Delaware's peach industry was hit hard by a ruinous blight known as "peach yellows" spread by aphids. In response to the loss of four million trees, Delaware orchardists, of necessity, shifted to other crops. Growers diversified with such substitutes as apples, strawberries, and blueberries. This change in farming practices helped create a more resilient agricultural system and allowed the state economy to recover from the devastating impact. *Jehu Reed mansion etching collection of Delaware Historical Society; apple picking tool collection of Milford Museum; peach sorting machine collection Delaware Agricultural Museum; Winslow Homer "Picking Peaches in Delaware" collection Cleveland Museum of Art.*

Page 31 Clayton & Transportation

Maryland took a contrary strategic step in 1825 to control rail traffic throughout the tri-state peninsula. The Annapolis legislature allocated funds for constructing a 141-mile rail line. The route was to run from Elkton, at the head of the Chesapeake Bay, south to Crisfield.

Meanwhile, newly elected Delaware Secretary of State Clayton recognized the potential negative impact of his neighbor's aggressive rail project. He knew a line on Maryland's eastern shore portion could divert trade, revenue, and funding from Delaware's future. Motivated by keen political instincts, the 32-year-old lawyer urgently sought out counterplans to safeguard Delaware's interests.

An 1827 financial depression forced Maryland backers to abandon their project. Railroad fever subsided, yet Clayton's outlook remained unshaken. He continued to dream of a Philadelphia-to-Norfolk line running north-south down Delaware's center. Maryland's political pressure alleviated, Clayton shifted his ambitions to the national stage, becoming a US Senator in 1829. He served on national committees such as Military Affairs, Militia, and Post Office and chaired the Judiciary Committee for two Congressional sessions.

However, the senator's years weren't without challenges. By 1835, his idealistic instincts clashed with Washington's in-fighting. Disillusioned with the national political scene, Clayton resigned in 1836. He resumed his private citizen pursuit of a long-sought Delaware railroad.

Still a young man, the 40-year-old harnessed his diverse life experiences to navigate the corridors of power and implement his vision. He got busy and single-handedly wrote a comprehensive charter proposal to the legislature for the "Delaware Railroad," requesting: 1) freedom from all manner of taxation for 50 years; 2) extensive powers of condemnation; 3) perpetual tax exemption for private land donated for rights-of-way; 4) state-funded survey costs and pre-organization expenses; and 5) a $25,000 subscription. The legislature, captivated by Clayton's charisma, granted the charter with only minimal changes.

Now, the Delaware Railroad was launched. Political heavyweights William Waples and Richard Mansfield joined the team, and proved vital in determining the railroad's route. The collaborators got busy superintending a thorough survey of the proposed right of way, scrutinizing the terrain, potential hurdles, and engineering challenges.

The survey supplied essential data for 1) constructing the railroad; 2) enabling effective planning; 3) resource allocation. However, the planning encountered unanticipated setbacks. Skeptical farmers, bank failures, and insufficient private donor subscriptions ultimately caused the project's demise. The three commissioners lost their charter. Delaware's north-south railway prospect was deferred for another 17 years.

These progressive businessmen nevertheless had laid the groundwork for a transformative transportation infrastructure. John M. Clayton was not to be denied his place in history. Future generations would come to recognize his efforts as a cornerstone moment in Delaware's economic growth and development.

Page 32 Moors

Attitudes towards slavery in Delaware became increasingly divided in the first half of the 19th century. The state's acceptance of the coexistence of free blacks and slaves stirred further unrest. Sussex County plantation owners feared slave uprisings, with the memory of Virginia's armed 1831 Nat Turner's Rebellion still fresh in their minds. In response, Delaware passed a law in 1832 to prevent just such an occurrence. This enactment transformed racial identity into a legal issue. Despite the underlying entanglement of Moors in these racial tensions, their lineage had been generally accepted. Nevertheless, questions and disputes over their ancestry began to surface.

Some white residents of Millsboro grew progressively skeptical of Levin Sockum, a successful Delaware Moor. Jealous shopkeeper competitors saw the 1832 statute as a means to sideline his country store business. When Sockum sold both ammunition and weapons to his cousin Isaiah Harmon, they took their chances, and sued him. The 1857 charge reads: "If any one person shall sell or loan any firearm to any negro or mulatto, he shall be deemed guilty and fined twenty dollars."

Levin Sockum called as one of his witnesses Lydia Clark, a highly respected 87 year old elder of the Moors, whom Sockum knew was thoroughly familiar with the tribe's true origins. He confidently believed she would clear his name. However, she was a renter living at the time on a white plantation owner's property and feared that if she told the story accurately, she would be dumped. Instead, she surprised her tribe by telling the jury that Moors were simply a racial mix of black and Native American. Based on Clark's testimony, then, Sockum was a mulatto, and therefore guilty. He was fined $20.

Lydia Clark's inability to uplift her community contrasted starkly with Isaac Harmon's post-Civil War Moor initiatives. Harmon was the wealthiest landowner in the Indian River community. He is remembered for standing up to the Delaware legislature, who in 1875 attempted to classify both Moors and Native Americans as 'colored'. This designation would force the education-oriented Moors to attend substandard colored schools.

Harmon successfully petitioned the General Assembly in 1881 for the establishment of "The Indian River School Districts for a Certain Class of Colored Persons," otherwise known as the Incorporated Body. This allowed Moors and Native Americans to create their own school. He went on to become a leader of the 1880s Nanticoke separatist movement.

Sussex County constructed two schools segregated for people of color. Moors who had not joined the Incorporated Body still had to attend Warwick #1 School (along with black and Native American students). Members of the Incorporated Body attended the Warwick Moors Colored School near Millsboro exclusively, shown in the school building photo.

Levin Sockum's trial first brought the Moors' struggle to the broader attention of Delawareans at large. However, Isaac Harmon's efforts in establishing his clan's school districts, in time, paved the way for a more inclusive future. His advocacy for the rights of the Moor community laid the foundation for greater acceptance and understanding of their unique heritage. *Photos: Delaware Public Archives; Sockum: "A Photographic Survey of the Indian River Community," 1977, Frank W. Porter III*

Page 33 Bethel Shipyards

Bethel, together with Wilmington, Smyrna, and Milford, was a prominent Victorian-era Delaware shipbuilding center. The town, originally founded as Lewisville in 1840, is strategically located on the Nanticoke River with easy access to the Chesapeake Bay and valuable timber reserves.

Jonathan M.C. Moore focused Bethel's drydock business around a unique schooner style known as the 'Chesapeake ram,' 'sailing ram,' or 'Nanticoke ram.' These vessels were specifically designed to navigate the narrow C&D Canal, optimize cargo capacity and maximize speed, all to conform with the canal's constraints. Moore, part-owner of the Bethel Marine Railway, served as superintendent of the shipbuilder for 42 years.

The completion of the transcontinental railroad in 1869 spurred significant growth in Bethel. Shipwrights valued the cedar sourced from Oregon, delivered via the new rail line. The timber's lightweight properties were prized for building masts on fast, cargo-carrying ships.

The town changed its name to Bethel in 1880 to distinguish itself from neighboring Lewes. The new name, which translates from "House of God" in Hebrew, reflects the community's strong Methodist influence. Now widely known for a flourishing ship repair and construction industry, Bethel must have indeed felt blessed during this period. From 1871 to 1918, the town's shipyards produced as many as thirty of these specialized schooners.

The Bethel Marine Railway in 1918 secured a federal contract to construct two government barges. However, the US Shipping Board (now the US Maritime Commission) unexpectedly and abruptly canceled the deal. Unbeknownst to Bethel shipyards, the US Army Corps of Engineers planned, the following year, to widen and deepen the C&D Canal. Oncoming diesel-powered ships gained access and were more competitive, hastening the Chesapeake ram's obsolescence.

Page 34 First Iron Shipbuilders in USA

Betts, Pusey, and Harlan's first venture into the shipbuilding industry, work on the 'Bangor,' a passenger and freight service ship, began in October 1843. Unfortunately, its career was marked by disaster. After a mishap during the launching, the 'Bangor' made a trial run trip to Cape May, NJ, traveling 10.61 miles an hour. However, on its second trip from Boston in July 1845, it caught fire and was beached on the coast of Castine, ME.

Betts, Pusey, and Harlan changed its name in 1841 to Betts, Harlan & Hollingsworth when Elijah Hollingsworth bought out Samuel Pusey. The new partnership quickly expanded operations. For a dozen years, Wilmington produced more iron tonnage in shipbuilding than any other US city. After Betts left the firm, Harlan & Hollingsworth grew to become the largest shipbuilder in Wilmington.

By 1887, the corporation expanded from an initial 2-acre shipyard to 43 acres on both banks of the Christiana River. They boasted a patented dry dock capable of accommodating a 340-foot long vessel. Within 40 years of the 'Bangor's' 1844 launch, the company had constructed 232 vessels worldwide, including 3 'monitors' for the government during the Civil War. *Bangor illustration, shipyard illustration, both Library of Congress*

Page 35 Hiding Sam at Corbit House

"My father, being a Quaker, was known to be of those to whom the terrified black man came to be helped into Pennsylvania and farther north, where he would be free," related his daughter Mary Corbit Warner years later.

"One bright spring morning while my father was absent, my mother quite alone in the old home was surprised to be asked to see a colored man who had come to our kitchen.

" 'Oh Mistus,' he exclaimed, 'please save me, I am a slave and because I was to be sold and sent far away from my wife and children, I run away hopin' to git to Pennsylvania. The sheriff and blood hounds are on my track, please ma'am won't you hide me?'

"Quick as woman's wit always is, she told him to follow and led him to the attic of our hip roofed house. Through the small foot of the cuddy hole, she ordered him to pass. To do this he had to go in sideways, the opening was so small. The floor joists extended to the outer frame of the roof and on these she had him lie down, and not move or speak until she ordered him.

"Hardly had she gotten down stairs when she was confronted by three men, who proved to be the Sheriff and his posse. They politely asked to see Mr. Corbit, and finding he was not at home, explained they wished to capture a valuable slave worth $3,000. This man had been seen entering this house.

"My mother very quietly gave them permission to examine the house, following them and opening all closet doors, and any place they wished to see.

"When they reached the attic her knees trembled and her heart beat so violently, she feared the men must be conscious of her perturbation.

"One of them pointed to the odd little door under the eaves and laughingly said 'Well Sam could not crawl through that cuddy hole.'

"Being satisfied after their search, that it was not possible the slave could be in the house, they left, after most courteously thanking my mother and apologizing for giving her so much trouble.

"Taking food and a quilt to the attic, she made the poor, trembling, frightened slave as comfortable as possible in his narrow quarters.

"At dusk she told him to put on other clothes, and walked with him to the main or state road, leading to Pennsylvania.

"Giving him some money, she said goodbye. He fell on his knees, thanking her, and crying, asked God to bless this kind lady who was helping him to freedom.

"After he was safely in Pennsylvania, he had a letter sent to my mother full of gratitude for her aid in his distress in time of his great need, saying he hoped some day to get his wife and family to join him."

Mary Corbit Warner's account, first given as a speech to the Delaware Chapter of the Colonial Dames in 1914, was published by the historian William H. Williams in his 1996 book 'Slavery and Freedom in Delaware, 1639-1865.'

Page 36 Clayton's Buena Vista home

When it came to the Mexican-American War, John M. Clayton, a member of the Whig Party, held a staunchly opposing view, believing the conflict was unwarranted. However, in February 1847, Zachary Taylor emerged victorious at the "Battle of Buena Vista," garnering significant support for his presidential candidacy. Taylor's outsider status and nationalist views appealed to those who were disenchanted with the Whig Party.

Upon completion of his New Castle home, Clayton chose to name it after Taylor's victory, a clear signal of his backing for the newly-minted candidate. This move led to a fractured political friendship between Clayton and his former ally, Henry Clay. Despite Clay's pledge not to campaign if the party nominated Taylor, the general went on to win the Whig Party nomination and subsequently, the presidency.

After assuming office in March 1849, President Taylor appointed John M. Clayton as his Secretary of State, a testament to the political risk that Clayton had taken and his ultimate career success.

Clayton lept upon his new springboard with zealous advocacy, showing astute judgment within a year in conducting international diplomacy. He negotiated the Clayton-Bulwer Treaty with England, laying the foundation for the construction of the Panama Canal. The politically savvy Clayton foresaw the completion of this massive endeavor would revolutionize ocean transport. Likewise, his ongoing leadership simultaneously propelled forward the new world of railroad transport.

Page 37 DuPont Powder Mill explosion

On April 14, 1847, tragedy struck at the DuPont Powder Mill. A sudden flash ignited the building, engulfing it in flames and trapping the workers inside. As they escaped, their clothes, saturated with explosive dust, caught fire, adding to the devastation. The explosion killed 18 people and injured many more, with the force felt as far as 30 miles away in Philadelphia.

Charles du Pont, owner of DuPont, Bauday & Co., and his wife Ann lived on their estate "Louviers" across the Brandywine River from the powder mills. Despite their wealth and distance from the mills, they were not immune to the effects of the explosion.

In a letter to her cousin, Ann described the horror of that fateful morning, the damage to their home, and the impact on the surrounding community: "...yesterday morning, about six o'clock, we had the most awful explosion of the powder mills. I was not up. Mr. du Pont had just risen. To describe the horror of the scene would be impossible. It was a bright morning, one of those days when nature seems to be full of smiles. I was debating whether I would lose in sleep these sweet hours, or get up; in an instant, without the slightest warning, there came a shock that seemed so terrific in its nature that I could only compare it to the meeting of heaven and earth, it appeared not to be local but a crash of the world, our window sashes, chairs, ceiling all in the twinkling of an eye laid prostrate, the concussion, the breaking of glass, and furniture, the horrid reports of the powder, the flash and the sudden pressure of the atmosphere, with the bursting of the doors, all formed a combination of horrors that can only be surpassed by that awful day we have all yet to see.

"After the first instant of the explosion I looked up and found my husband pale and bleeding; it was, however, only a scratch from a piece of broken glass; he was pale from fear of his family on the other side [of the Brandywine River.] He knew not who was spared, yet a kind of Providence saved them all, though their houses are dreadfully shattered. We have but one habitable room and that is made so by carpets and blankets nailed to the windows and I have written this letter at 11 o'clock in the day by candlelight. The shrieks of the wives and children so soon made widows and orphans rose in sad succession to the preceding horror, human heads, arms and feet were found on that peaceful looking bank of the Brandywine where you and I have walked."

This incident was not the only disaster at DuPont's Powder Mill in the 19th century. An explosion in 1818 claimed the lives of 34 people, and another in 1890 resulted in 12 fatalities. *Powder label: collection Hagley Museum & Library; Louviers home: Delaware Public Archives*

Page 38 The Delaware Railroad

However, the challenge of raising capital remained, as the small populations in Kent and Sussex counties limited potential investors. To overcome this obstacle, Harrington assembled a board of directors primarily from these two counties and secured their investment. Despite this, the project stalled until 1852 when the state agreed to contribute funds, provided the board sold a total of 20,000 shares. Harrington's reputation and the board's local focus instilled trust in the people, allowing him to raise the necessary funds within a month. With the financial support secured, the dream of a railroad for southern Delaware was set to become a reality.

Page 39 Delaware State Fair

Delaware's first annual exhibit of modern farm practices took place in 1845 in Odessa, sponsored by the Agricultural Society of St. Georges and Appoquinimink Hundred (later the New Castle Agricultural Society).

Imagine the scene at the heart of the bustling fairgrounds. An expansive display of shiny farm tools captures the eye of every visitor. Further into the crowd, the livestock competition is in full swing, each proud farmer vying for the coveted trophy in a spectacle of agricultural prowess. Amidst the clamor, children huddle around a whimsical Punch & Judy puppet show, their laughter audible over the rhythmic snipping at the sheep-shearing demonstration.

Peter F. Causey, whose governorship began in 1854, understood that Delaware, being largely an agricultural state, could benefit from an annual statewide showcase. He stressed the importance of spreading know-how to the state's farmers. The fair could be a platform where exhibitors and townspeople alike could rub elbows and learn from each other.

Causey also saw the state fair as a boost for Delaware's economy. He wanted the fair to encourage farmers to step up their game and increase yields.

Understanding the potential of the expanded Delaware Railroad to widen travel reach, the 40th General Assembly in 1855 decided to time the fair with the railroad's expansion. It was all part of making Delaware shine.

When Governor Peter Causey backed the creation of an Agricultural Society in Kent County, these goals were at the forefront of his mind. The society got to work planning an early October fair in Dover.

A lot of things have changed since then, and today's Delaware State Fair is a full-blown spectacle of entertainment and exhibitions. But it all started back in 1855 with that first event in Dover's Fairview Park. *Fairgrounds photo collection of Delaware Public Archives*

Page 40 Lewes Country Doctor

David Hall, a highly esteemed physician, was appointed by the governor in 1879 as one of the seven founding members of Delaware's State Board of Health. He later served as the President of the Delaware State Medical Society, and by 1898, the *Morning News* [Wilmington] hailed him as "one of the most popular physicians of this state."

Dr. Hall remained committed to his patients, making house calls throughout his lifelong career. In January 1905, *The Evening Journal* [Wilmington] reported that, despite having passed the age of 70, Dr. Hall continued to tend to his patients, having seen as many as 50 of them in a single day.

The rigorous schedule proved too much for the elderly gentleman, who passed away soon thereafter. Dr. Hall achieved his desire to 'die in harness,' as he put it, never believing in retirement and remaining devoted to his community contributions until the end. *Doctor office and bag: collection Lewes Historical Society*

Page 41 Wilmington Reminiscences

"They drew a circle on the ice, and had a stone round but rather flat on one side, in size and shape much like an old-fashioned roll of tobacco; in this a handle was placed, by which it was pushed over the ice, something like pitching quoits.

"A dangerous sport practiced here in those days by a younger class was riding on a whirligig. A post was secured in the ice, with a hole in the top, through which a long pole was passed; a sled was attached to each end by a rope; on these the riders were seated, four or six men holding the middle of the pole, forced it round with such rapidity that a dense mist enveloped the whole circle.

"It is amusing to spectators who come here to witness the feats displayed in skating. Some with great dexterity cut ciphers and write letters, others have little girls holding on to their coats as they skate, or in sleds fastened to their waists, flying over the ice in full glee; many are skilled in the art of sliding a great distance, others are popping down at every attempt, yet not discouraged, so absorbed in pleasure they are regardless of the intense cold.

"Joyous as these sports may be, on some occasions they are mingled with sorrow. Thirty winters have gone since, on a fine morning, a few school girls came here at noon to slide; and, as there was water over the edge of the dam, they prudently declined to venture. A fearless one sprang on, the ice broke, and in a moment she was gone."

Montgomery, a prominent figure in Wilmington society during the first half of the 19th century, spent several years as an educator, running a sewing and drawing school for girls. She later co-founded the Female Bible Society.

Additionally, Montgomery played a crucial role in revitalizing Wilmington's Old Swedes Church. This Episcopalian place of worship, active since 1698, closed its doors following the 1830 Christmas service. The church's congregation had moved to the new Trinity Chapel in uptown Wilmington. The historic church remained neglected until Montgomery organized a fundraising campaign to restore it. Henrietta Allmond's generous bequest enabled the church's revitalization, and services resumed in 1842. The Old Swedes Church continues, to this day, to hold services. Elizabeth Montgomery was laid to rest in a distinguished location within the church's cemetery, a testament to her contributions. *Ice skates: collection Delaware Historical Society*

Page 42 Big Thursday

Before 1852, Delaware Bay watermen had the liberty to harvest oysters throughout the year without any restrictions. However, in 1852, the Delaware legislature expressed concerns about over harvesting and imposed a ban on oyster fishing from May to August 10th. From then on, the second Thursday of August became known as "Big Thursday."

"Oak Orchard, Sandy Land, Puddle Hole and Burton Island. This is where they assembled, " recalled 80 year old Dr. Blaine Adkins in a 1973 interview.

"Many would leave for the celebration on Wednesday evening," he continued, "in covered wagons, dearborns (which were a type of buggy), and carriages drawn by mules and horses. Fodder and corn was always taken along for the feeding of the animals."

The celebrations included traditional frolics with fiddle and banjo playing, dancing, and friendly rivalries among dancers. The evening would culminate in feasting on freshly caught fish, clams, crabs, and oysters cooked over wood fires on the beach.

"We always carried fried chicken and cooked beets and cucumbers," remembered Margaret Cordrey of Oak Orchard, in a 1972 *Delmarva News* item. "Had never heard of potato salad. We carried crackers and a big round cheese. We had homemade biscuits. Wasn't much bread sold around here then."

Dr. Adkins noted that swimming among all ages at Big Thursday was popular because of very shallow waters. Quote "Bathing suits were quite different from today, though, with shirt tops below the knees and stockings to cover the legs—one of these suits would make 100 bikini suits of today."

In response to 'Big Thursday,' which was understood to be a whites-only event, Delaware's black community created its own summer oyster celebration called "Black Saturday." This event would take place on the Saturday following Big Thursday and would draw a large crowd of both black and white attendees.

Over the years, the "Big Thursday" celebrations expanded to various beaches in lower Delaware. However, by 1959, over harvesting, oyster population decline, and the widespread use of cars had weakened the event's significance. *Photo collection of Bowers Beach Maritime Museum*

Page 43 Leipsic

Delaware's General Assembly briefly considered changing the town's moniker to Vienna in the early 19th century, but settled instead on Leipsic.

Leipsic had already gained renown as a crucial US hub for muskrat fur trading. The new name nodded to the German town of Leipsic (now "Leipzig"), likewise a major fur-shipping center. Despite the name's German roots, the community pronounces the town as "LIP-sig", veering away from "LEAP-sick", the traditional Teutonic pronunciation.

The fashionable popularity of muskrat fur ultimately diminished in America. Nevertheless, the international market, including countries such as China, Greece, Italy, Russia, and Korea, still demands this commodity.

Page 44 Diamond Matches

Edward Tatnall in 1853 established a small sulfur match factory along Wilmington's Brandywine Creek. The sulfur matches of the day were highly unstable, prone to accidental ignition, and caused numerous fires. A young Englishman named Henry C. Courtney worked for Tatnall and saw a business opportunity in this flaw. Moonlighting, he developed a safer product—the parlor or cracking match. Courtney's friction matches contained little or no sulfur, leading to better ignition.

Meanwhile, William H. Swift joined the firm to provide financial and clerical services in 1860. Unlike Tatnall, Swift recognized the new match as a game changer and deftly outmaneuvered Tatnall for control of the company. Tatnall's judgment was seemingly clouded regarding the true value of his enterprise. He sold the business to Swift in a fire sale for a mere $1,400 (equivalent to $50,000 today). While Courtney struck a match, Swift struck gold, and Tatnall flamed out.

Swift retained Courtney as his partner. The pair began producing the new match formula in 1861 under the name Diamond State Parlor Matches, inspired by Delaware's popular nickname. The timing was perfect. The Civil War created a match shortage due to disruptions in trade and resources.

The United States experienced a period of post-war pent-up demand, and the constraints created opportunities for various industries to thrive. By 1870, A. Beecher & Sons of New Haven, CT had introduced the Beecher Machine, an innovative device that automated the process of matchstick production. This advancement pushed Swift & Courtney to seek a merger with their competitor or be left in the dust.

The merged company, Swift & Courtney & Beecher, incorporated in New Haven in 1880 as the Diamond Match Company. When Henry C. Courtney passed away in 1886, his fortune was worth an impressive $1,500,000 (over $47 million today).

Page 45 Rehoboth Beach Beginnings

The Delaware legislature incorporated the "Rehoboth Hotel Company" (RHC) in 1855, reserving five acres of state land for commercial development. Even so, the endeavor's specific location remained in flux until 1869.

Striving to reach the beach, the railroads lagged in tandem with RHC. They still needed a decade to develop their track networks. Seeing the untapped passenger opportunity, Delaware RR, the Philadelphia, Wilmington & Baltimore RR, and the Junction & Breakwater RR all vied to be the first to establish a presence at this growing seaside attraction.

Beach construction started in earnest in the late 1860s, with businessman Louis Frederick arriving in Rehoboth in 1869. He established a "small place of entertainment" at the head of Rehoboth Bay.

The Methodist Episcopal Church's combined Wilmington, Philadelphia, Baltimore, and Washington Annual Conferences created the Rehoboth Beach Camp Meeting Association in 1872. The M.E. group secured several hundred acres on the northern shore of Rehoboth Bay. They envisioned a camp-meeting facility to "provide and maintain a seaside resort, where everything inconsistent with Christian morality as taught by the church, shall be excluded and prohibited."

The Methodists hired contractor William Foulk, who built the 50-room, 4-story Surf House in 1873, surrounded by seven cottages. The Delaware Railroad constructed a link from Lewes. The state set up a new post office. Both activities happened that fall.

Three-quarters of a mile south of the Methodist property, Wilmington developer George W. Bright carved out his turf with construction of the Bright House. Positioned right on the beach, this 1875 establishment provided 73 "sleeping rooms" and, at capacity, could house 200 guests.

Dover's William C. Fountain erected the adjacent 3-story Douglass House in 1877. The new addition offered guests billiards and card tables. Wilmington's *News Journal* snickered that "nearly all of the [fun lovers were] attracted by those 'good things' which Rehoboth Beach [Camp Meeting Association] ... does not supply."

A hotel assemblage, a selection of 'boarding tents,' a variety of rental cottages, and the post office all shaped what later became the boardwalk's southern terminus. At this time the cluster was known as 'Rehoboth City'. 'Rehoboth Beach,' to the north, pertained only to the Methodist camp meeting development.

The Junction & Breakwater Railroad extended to the camp meeting grounds in 1878. Just three years later, the Methodist church, disturbed by nearby 'dens of sins,' pulled their investments. However, not all departed. The stalwarts, along with fresh investors, rebranded themselves as the "Rehoboth Beach Association."

The Queen Anne's Railroad in 1884 ran a line down the main avenue of the newly merged Rehoboth City-Rehoboth Beach environs. Their newest depot - 'Rehoboth Beach.' It was only a matter of time before a boardwalk appeared.

Rehoboth Beach's growth, unlike neighboring Lewes, did not materialize around a natural harbor. Instead, the emergence of a leisure-rich middle class propelled its development. The "Rehoboth Hotel Company" incorporation in 1855 hints at planning, but the town's evolution primarily stemmed from a myriad of competitive decisions made by railroads, land developers, and the Methodist Camp Meeting Association. *Postcard collection of Delaware Public Archives; Model train collection of Zwannendael Museum*

Page 46 Harriet Tubman and the Tilly Escape

Harriet Tubman, famed conductor of the Underground Railroad, made at least 19 trips from Dorchester County, MD to the South between 1850 and 1860. Her courageous efforts liberated 300 slaves, none of which were ever recaptured. Abolitionist friends affectionately nicknamed her "General Tubman" in honor of Tubman's heroic leadership.

Tubman accepted a daring assignment in October 1856: to assist a slave named Tilly with her broad-daylight and very public escape from Baltimore.

The Chesapeake Bay journey required Tilly to possess a bond or freedom certificate, one of many obstacles. Tubman's connection with the steamboat 'Kent' captain, who had helped her once before, facilitated obtaining these crucial shipboard papers.

Subsequently, the two women boarded a Baltimore-Seaford line. The ticket clerk pulled the two aside. Panic set in! "Oh Lord," prayed Tubman once the clerk was out of earshot. "You've been with me in six troubles, don't desert me in the seventh!"

The suspicious clerk circled back with the captain's approval in hand and grudgingly allowed the two women to stay aboard. Once they reached Seaford, Tubman and Tilly trudged to the town's only hotel for supper and a good night's rest.

A slave trader eyed them in the hotel lobby the next morning. Tubman knew full well he held the legal power to capture them and send them back South in shackles. When the slave catcher demanded to know their identities, Tubman confidently presented the captain's certificate. After a moment's hesitation, he backed off.

They forged ahead, walking eight miles to Bridgeville, and caught a train from there to Camden. William Brinkley, a free black man, met them there. He transported the two by carriage to Wilmington, a distance of 50 miles.

Finally, at journey's end, Underground Railroad leader Thomas Garrett received them at his Philadelphia home, where Tilly reunited with her fiancé.

Tilly's flight remains the sole documented instance of Harriet Tubman leading an operation from the headwaters of the Nanticoke. In 2013, the National Park Service included this dramatic escape route on the National Underground Railroad Network to Freedom trail. *Harriet Tubman display courtesy of Seaford Museum; Quilt, collection of Delaware Agricultural Museum*

Page 47 Scrapple

Scrapple, a dish made from pig parts, cornmeal and/or buckwheat flour, and spices, may seem like a 20th-century invention. However, the dish's origins trace back to the 17th century, when German Palatinate immigrants brought it to Pennsylvania.

The term "scrapple" comes from an intriguing translation of the German phrase "panhas kreppel," which literally means "pan rabbit donut." To understand this connection, consider that a donut is made from a slice of dough. Early German immigrants in America referred to the dish as "panhas," and the modifier "kreppel" came to signify a slice of food. The "s" at the end of "panhas" joined the beginning of "kreppel" to make the new word "scrapple."

The word "scrapple" first appeared in quotes in 1860s Delaware newspaper articles, as a colloquial shorthand for "a slice of panhas." Within two decades, the quotes were dropped, and the modern spelling of the term was established. *Photo location: 1890s farmhouse of Delaware Agricultural Museum*

Page 48 Confederates in Delaware

The division of Delaware during the Civil War could be clearly seen in Georgetown's Public Square and Circle, where the Brick Hotel and the nearby Eagle Hotel each attracted sympathizers from the opposing side.

"One local folk tale concerning the [Brick]," says its National Register of Historic Places application, "centers on its reputation as a favorite lounging spot for staunch supporters of the Union cause at a time when the county was leaning toward the Confederate cause in public opinion.

"The southern sympathizers in the area were in the habit of spending their evenings in the barroom of the Eagle Hotel and elsewhere on the Public Square and Circle. Late in the evening when both sides had had their fill, tradition says that they piled out of their respective refuges and fought out their differences in the middle of the Circle.

"In view of the political climate in Sussex County during the Civil War the story is quite possibly true."

During the Civil War, Delaware was deemed a Union state; however, the reality on the ground was significantly more complex. Envision the Brick Hotel/Eagle Hotel incident transpiring in, say, Massachusetts or Georgia. The skirmish in the circle would have unfolded only once, rather than recurrently, night after night. One faction would have been slain, injured, or driven from the town.

The Confederate Monument in Georgetown stands as the sole memorial in the US commemorating Delawareans who fought for the South. It bears 95 names, although it is estimated that 2,000 to 3,000 Delawareans actually enlisted in the Confederate army.

On the Union side, Delaware contributed 8 regiments (comprising 3,200 soldiers), a cavalry battalion (with 300-1,000 soldiers), and a battery (of 100 soldiers). The number of Union soldiers exceeded that of the Confederate, true, but not by an insurmountable majority.
Georgetown aerial photo courtesy Delaware Public Archives

Page 49 Fort Delaware, Civil War Prison

Before long, tens of thousands of prisoners rendered the overcrowded 70-acre facility a veritable chamber of horrors. Pacifists labeled Fort Delaware 'The Andersonville of the North,' protesting the US Army penitentiary's equally shocking treatment of prisoners.

Delaware's state legislature, in May 1813, transferred control of the island to the federal government. The US Army then stationed a company of 100-200 men there, serving as a defensive outpost for Philadelphia. The island received its first Confederate prisoners of war following the 1862 Shenandoah Valley Battle of Kernstown. Subsequently, Delaware troops transported 250 members of Stonewall Jackson's Army to the island.

The Union garrison sheltered these prisoners in wooden barracks on Pea Patch, not within the fort itself. The constant influx of new prisoners rapidly led to overcrowding, and by June 1863, the island quartered 8,000 inmates. Fort commander General Albin Francisco Schoepf expanded the barracks to house 10,000 prisoners.

Even so, Gettysburg, bloodiest battle of the entire war, occurred less than a month later, and prisoner count surged. From General James J. Archer down to the lowest-ranking private, all crammed into Fort Delaware. By August, the island's population swelled to 12,500 prisoners.

Conditions at the fort were far from ideal, with some prisoners receiving better care than others. Nevertheless, prisoners' letters suggest that the situation might not have been entirely bleak. For instance, T. Sumpter Belvin, a soldier from Company A, 11th Georgia Infantry, wrote to his mother on March 1, 1864, that the 'sick are receiving better care than they did in Dixie.' His mother wept while reading the letter and said, 'that was his way of getting a letter through the lines; I know the Yankees made him say that!' Blevin died at the fort. He was buried in a grave with 5 others.

And on March 23, Missourian Edwin S. Johnson writes to his sister: "I have written about all that I am permitted to write." It was wartime. Letters were screened.

Food rations were scarce, and prisoners often went hungry. Captain James Bosang of Company C, 4th Virginia Infantry, recalled his experience in the latter half of 1864, when his rations were insufficient and barely edible. "I was hungry for five months, day and night; our rations consisted of a slice of baker's bread about 1-¼" thick or two or three crackers with a small slice of pickled pork, a cup of weak coffee and at dinner time about the same amount of bread and a cup of soup or greasy water, in which occasionally a bean or two would be found, but mostly seasoned with flies."

The United States Sanitary Commission's official report from a Commission of Inquiry relentlessly painted a more positive picture, claiming that prisoners were well-fed and supplied with fresh vegetables.

Historians have criticized Brigadier General Albin A. Schoepf, a recent German immigrant and career soldier in charge of the facility. His harsh handling of the prison seemed far outside the accepted international rules of engagement. Twenty-seven hundred prisoners perished under his watch. *Barracks photo courtesy National Park Service; soldiers marching illustration: Harpers Weekly courtesy Delaware Historical Society*

Page 50 Annie Jump Cannon

The future renowned astronomer was captivated as a child by the night sky. She observed the heavens through a small attic window and recorded her findings in a notebook by candlelight. Young Annie's mother often taught her about constellations and star names.

Wilmington Conference Academy of Dover accepted Cannon for early college enrollment. She studied there till 1880. The 17-year-old then matriculated to Wellesley College, graduating as valedictorian in 1884. She later enrolled in Radcliffe Women's College at Harvard as a "special student" to pursue spectroscopy. While at Radcliffe, Cannon mentored under Edward C. Pickering, the director of the Harvard College Observatory. He kept her on at his observatory, where Cannon participated in, and eventually led, Pickering's star cataloging project, beginning in 1885. She remained at Harvard College Observatory for 44 years.

Pickering sought to organize stars based on their temperature and spectral type. Dr. Cannon documented 400,000 celestial bodies, five novae, one double star, and discovered over 300 variable stars (She could reportedly catalog up to three stars a minute!). Her system, known as the Harvard Classification Scheme, is still in use today. The Henry Draper catalog published Annie Jump Cannon's findings across nine volumes. In 1931, the National Academy of Sciences honored this world-famous astronomer for her star-studded accomplishments.

Dr. Annie Jump Cannon, despite being legally deaf, broke several professional barriers. She was the first woman to be awarded an honorary doctorate from Oxford. Likewise, she became the first woman elected as an officer of the American Astronomical Society. The AAS established the Annie Jump Cannon Award in her memory. It is given annually to a North American woman astronomer for distinguished contributions to astronomy or related sciences. *Photo collection of Delaware Historical Society*

Page 51 1863 Draft in Smyrna

A draftee could "furnish an acceptable substitute" for themselves if they could find one. For instance, a wealthy individual could send an indentured servant.

Moreover, the new conscription treated volunteers the same as draftees. Both received equal pay and the new bill removed any sign-up bounty. Patriotic citizens had no incentive to volunteer.

In early April, Lincoln decided to make the first draft calls from "states deficient under the last call." Delaware had sent a notably large number of men to serve in 1861-2, and had a credit at the War Department for 8,743 men.

Protests began long before Delaware's next draft round in July. The *Smyrna Times* reported in mid-April on a secret organization in Berks County, PA, just over the border from Delaware, "whose main object seems to be the resistance of the draft. They would try the constitutionality of the conscription act, and, failing that, use force." Its four leaders were arrested on conspiracy charges.

In early May, Lincoln closed a loophole in the draft bill that initially exempted non-citizen immigrants from serving. *The Smyrna Times* commented on these residents who, having previously stated their intent to become citizens, "now wish to escape the coming draft, and claim to be pure and unadulterated foreigners. The President is after these gentry with a very sharp stick," said the paper.

In early June, the *Smyrna Times* reported that "a number of young men of New Castle County of secesh [ed. 'secessionist'] proclivities are leaving for parts unknown. Five young men of the Cochran family left Middletown a few days ago for Canada to avoid the enrollment and did not intend to return until the draft had concluded."

As the registration deadline approached in early July, eight men were arrested for 'attacking the house' of John Green, enrolling officer for Murderkill Hundred, according to the *Weekly Delaware State Journal and Statesman*. The paper also reported that Samuel Draper, the enrolling officer for Milford Hundred, had encountered some trouble in carrying out his duties. He went to the residence of one John Wesley Hall to discuss enrollment. Hall ordered Draper off his farm and threatened violence. As Draper turned to leave, Hall yelled out that if he went further down the "neck," "he would catch it." Hall's wife threw eggs at Draper as he fled. The two were promptly arrested.

Although Delaware's towns never erupted into open riots like New York City did in July, pockets of resistance persisted throughout the summer. "From what we can judge in conversation with people from all parts of the county," said the *Georgetown Messenger* in late August, "nearly all who can by any possible means raise $300, will do so. There seems to be a disposition on the part of those called to remain at home."

Lincoln's suspension of habeas corpus in late September sent shock waves across the Union. Newspaper tones shifted, and commentaries mocking draft dodgers emerged. *The Union* [Georgetown] reported in early November that "a number of bachelors, over thirty-five, were drafted in Providence. On being laughed at for not being married, and thereby escaping the draft, they maliciously replied: 'Better to serve three years than for life!'"

By December, Lincoln achieved the troop enrollments he sought. "The avails of the draft so far as ascertained up to this time," reported the *Delaware State Journal* on December 15, "are 60,000 men [nationwide] and $12,000,000 spent."

Lincoln's decision to suspend habeas corpus was undoubtedly severe and possibly unconstitutional. However, it provided him with the necessary leverage to persuade reluctant potential soldiers to join his army. In time, Delaware followed suit with the other states. As historian Scharf concluded, "The proportion of soldiers given by the little Diamond State to uphold the flag of the Republic was equal to, if not greater than, that of any other State." Patience was simply required. *Draft wheel photo: collection of Delaware Historical Society*

Page 52 Heptasophs and the life insurance industry

The original Order of Heptasophs was founded in New Orleans in 1852, becoming one of the country's earliest fraternal benefit organizations. The group's name, derived from the Greek roots meaning "seven" and "wise," represents the seven wise men. According to its charter, the order was established by a few earnest, unselfish individuals for fraternal and beneficial purposes. Heptasoph teachings aimed at strengthening members' character and elevating their moral principles.

"Philadelphia appears to be the Paradise of secret orders," clucked the *Delaware Tribune* in 1869. The Heptasophs had just held their national conclave in Philadelphia and boasted 500 lodges across the country. However, the fraternity did not receive much attention from Delaware newspapers for another decade.

The 1870s marked a profound transformation in the purpose of the Heptasophs, as well as countless other secret societies originally established as social clubs. The Civil War had exposed the fragility of life, leading to a surge in 'beneficiary' secret societies that offered sick, funeral, and death benefits to members.

In 1878, the Improved Order of Heptasophs (IOH) split from the original order due to a disagreement over offering life insurance. The IOH reflected the growing trend of late 19th-century fraternal orders becoming involved in the life insurance business. According to the charter of the new group, "The main object of the association is to secure a fund of from $1,000 to $5,000 to the beneficiary of a deceased member."

The Zeta Conclave of Baltimore formed the core of the IOH splinter group. Zeta's C.E. Baird in 1879 organized the Diamond Conclave in Dover. The new group, Delaware's first IOH conclave, participated in an October 1880 fraternal organizations Baltimore parade. They marched alongside more familiar names such as the Odd Fellows and the Knights of Pythias.

Over time, the IOH increasingly resembled an insurance company rather than a fraternity. By 1915, Delaware's Friendship Conclave No. 1 of the Heptasophs or Seven Wise Men, Inc. had failed to pay taxes for the preceding two years, resulting in the repeal of its charter by Governor Richard McMullen. Facing financial struggles nationwide, the IOH merged with the Fraternal Aid Union in May 1917, which subsequently changed its name to Standard Life Association. *Photo Red Man's Hall collection Delaware Historical Society*

Page 53 Morocco Leather

Alfred P. Stevenson's career path embodies the fluctuating fortunes of the Morocco Leather finishing industry, rising and falling in sync with the industry's own trajectory.

Stevenson, fresh out of law school in 1872, was full of future optimism. His uncle, John G. Baker, the founder of the John G. Baker Company, dropped an offer in his lap. The 5-year-old Wilmington-based company quickly ascended to prominence in Morocco Leather finishing.

The Workingmen's Loan Association board of directors in 1880 elected Stevenson to join them. This invitation set him on a path towards becoming a visible figure in the business world. Superintendent Stevenson in 1884 represented the John G. Baker Company at the Morocco Manufacturers National Exchange's 38th semi-annual meeting.

Stevenson's active involvement in his community was evidenced by his role as a trustee of the Second Baptist Church. Further demonstrating his commitment, he contributed a large stained-glass window to the church's new chapel. Additionally, he generously funded the construction of a house of worship for the Baptist City Mission.

John G. Baker incorporated his company in 1893 and changed its name to Baker Leather Company. He brought on Alfred P. Stevenson and Charles W. Gouert as additional incorporators. Despite rumors of financial troubles, the company held steady. Meanwhile, the broader Morocco Leather industry faced numerous challenges. The market ran up against changing fashion trends, imitation products, competition from imported goat skins and labor disputes.

The unexpected death of Baker in 1895, at the age of 62, left Stevenson and Gouert at significant crossroads. Gouert decided to step away from the industry. Stevenson opted to sell the struggling company. He founded the Stevenson Leather Company the same year with additional capital.

Despite Stevenson's new plans, the business went downhill fast. He exhausted investor funds. Stockholders became disgruntled. Dover's Chancery Court in 1898 placed the Stevenson Leather Company in receivership. Soon after, the Importers and Traders Bank of New York filed a petition to declare Stevenson bankrupt. Although the court dismissed his case due to technicalities, the incident tarnished Stevenson's reputation and alienated potential new investors.

Stevenson used his unencumbered assets to establish the Diamond Leather Company in 1900, yet, a looming financial predicament overshadowed any remaining ambitions. The following year, auctioneers put the factory headquarters on the block, and Stevenson disappeared from public view.

Over the next 19 years, Stevenson's name only surfaced when his properties went up for sheriff's sales. Weighty circumstances forced him to abandon an opulent Wilmington mansion. A humbled man moved a final time to Penny Hill, DE, where he died in 1920. *Traveler's Guide cover collection of Zwaanendael Museum*

Page 54 Richard Allen founds A.M.E. Church

After Sturgis dealt this heart-wrenching family betrayal, the young Allen felt, even more, the chains of bondage weigh him down. For a time, he lost faith in the possibility of freedom. Despite this harsh setback, Allen's trust in God remained steadfast.

In 1777, Allen experienced a call to religion and attended a series of Methodist revivals. He soon became an important figure among the local African American Methodist community. He learned to read and write through the Methodist Society and uncovered a real knack for preaching. Stokely Sturgis, noticing this, began to encourage Richard Allen to conduct prayers and preach in his house.

Allen depicted the start of his spiritual journey: "I was brought to see myself poor, wretched and undone. Shortly after, I obtained mercy through the blood of Christ."

In 1779, the itinerant Methodist preacher, Freeborn Garrettson, delivered a sermon titled "Thou Art Weighed in the Balance and Found Wanting" at the Sturgis plantation. His impassioned claim that slaveholders would face eternal damnation for their inhumanity had a profound effect on Sturgis, stirring his troubled conscience. Shortly thereafter, Sturgis approached Richard Allen and his brother, offering them the chance to buy their own freedom. The price he proposed was either 60 pounds in gold and silver, or $2,000 in Continental currency.

Stokely Sturgis was among the first to convert under Allen's ministry, following Allen's formal licensure and ordination to preach a year later. Francis Asbury, who founded the first Methodist church in America, personally initiated Allen into his calling.

Allen was keen to fulfill the terms of the agreed upon manumission as promptly as possible. He understood if Sturgis, then in his sixties, were to pass away before the debt was paid, he and his brother would be "sold to the highest bidder," given Sturgis's significant debts.

Allen was expected to continue his previous tasks working in the farm's fields, planting flax, corn, and wheat. Only then did Sturgis permit him to seek out additional jobs chopping wood and laboring in a brickyard. As another sideline, Allen also hauled salt for George Washington's troops from Rehoboth Beach. Richard Allen's hustling enabled him to purchase his freedom a year and a half before the stipulated 5.

In a telling gesture of his character, Allen presented the still struggling Sturgis with 18-½ bushels of salt, worth a guinea per bushel at the time, in consideration of the "uncommon Kind treatment of his Master during his Servitude." Allen spoke of Sturgis as a "very tender, humane man."

This gift was no small token: on the contrary, the salt's value was at least half a year's wages for a working man of the time. Sturgis, in return, testified to Allen's good character in Allen's "freedom papers" of 1781: he "Beheaved himself Soberly and Honostly when he wrought about this place." Reverend Allen began his circuit riding ministry up and down Delmarva shortly thereafter.

The young preacher subsequently moved to the Society Hill neighborhood of Philadelphia, and by 1793, had founded Bethel African Methodist Episcopal Church. Today, Richard Allen's church boasts a global membership of approximately 2.5 million members, making it one of the largest Methodist denominations in the world.

Page 55 Faux Latin Poem

The allegedly rediscovered Latin poem appeared in two college periodicals, stirring controversy. When friend Samuel Bancroft sent Smithers' poem to the *New York Herald*, accusing Harte of plagiarism, the joke turned bitter.

Smithers, a Lafayette College alumnus, shared the "ancient" poem with Professor Lyman Coleman. Duped, Coleman published it in 1871. Franklin & Marshall's magazine also featured it in 1873 after Smithers met alumni Bancroft and William F. Smalley.

The scandal, reported by *The New York Times*, extended beyond Delaware with angry letters from across the nation. A New England journal eventually exposed the poem as a hoax by a Harte admirer.

The New York Times noted the debacle could've been avoided had anyone noticed Smithers' typeset disclaimer: "Bret Harte's poems, put into Latin verse by N.B. Smithers..."

Today, the Harry Ransom Center, University of Texas/Austin, holds Harte's papers, including a letter from Smithers to Bancroft, dated April 1, 1886—April Fools Day—wittily gifting the original handwritten version of his poem.

Page 56 Sleighs

Delawareans had already been using sleigh bells for over a century when the Victorians introduced "Jingle Bells" (1857) and Currier & Ives prints depicted cheerful young couples riding in fashionable 'cutters'.

The *Smyrna Times* reported in February 1858 that the town reverberated with the sound of sleigh bells from morning to night, as "flashy turnouts dashed through the streets at breakneck speeds".

Eric Sloane, in "The Seasons of America Past," states that sleigh bells began as folded metal around 1750 and evolved into the popular American sleigh bell around 1800. These bells were manufactured and distributed globally from East Hampton, CT, known as "Jingle-town."

By the late 19th century, Delaware's winter newspapers were filled with advertisements for sleigh bells, including Swiss Pole Chimes, King Henry Bells, and Mikado Chimes.

The *Delaware Tribune* reported on February 13, 1868, that the sleighing in the Delaware City area had never been finer. The constant jingle of sleigh bells "filled the air as wealthy and leisurely men enjoyed the company of delighted belles within the sleighs". But whether it was the wealthy enjoying leisurely rides, or the working class going about their daily chores, everyone utilized sleighs to traverse the snow-covered landscapes.

Sleighs with bells persisted into the 20th century. Some Delawareans still fondly reminisce about their grandparents' use of the riggings. Once Alfred I. du Pont purchased his first automobile in 1899, however, Delaware's winter transportation would never sound the same. *Sleigh: collection Lewes History Museum; Bells: collection Harrington Historical Society; Lap robe: collection Marvel Carriage Museum*

Page 57 Quinby and his flying machine

"We hardly think he will be able to compete with the swallows in this harness," remarked a June 24, 1871 *Scientific American* article. "We would suggest starting from a low point initially, so that, in case of a fall, the impact would be less severe."

Watson Fell Quinby had crafted a bat-like contraption, intended to be powered by the pilot's legs and steered with his arms. Quinby kept his activity under wraps and secretly did the construction in his Newport, DE carriage house.

He hauled the clumsy thing to the roof of his building and donned a skin-tight suit. Quinby adjusted his invention and leaped into the air, only to realize that foot-power was insufficient to keep the daredevil device aloft. His family rescued him from the machine's wreckage. Fortunately, he sustained no serious injuries.

Quinby patented several ideas for flying machines, including an 'Apparatus for navigating air' in 1867, a 'Flying machine' in 1869, a 'Flying apparatus' in 1872, and an 'Aerial ship' in 1879. None of these 'ornithopters' ever went airborne.

Watson Fell Quinby's story serves as a testament to the value of perseverance in the face of failure. Though he did not achieve personal success in manned flight, his relentless experimentation and documentation played a crucial role in the eventual realization of human flight. His pioneering spirit continues to inspire present and future generations of aviators and innovators.

Page 58 Lifesaving Stations

Just before midnight on March 11th, the southeast wind suddenly veered to the northwest, bringing with it rain, sleet, and snow, and blowing with a hurricane's strength. The turbulent waters and the raging storm, amidst the pitch-black night, would have struck fear into even the bravest heart.

As daylight broke on the morning of March 12th, the Lewes Station keeper gathered his crew, knowing their services would be needed. However, the gale's force was so immense that the sand and sleet battered their faces, forcing them to crawl back to the station.

Half an hour later, the weather momentarily calmed, and the surfmen set out once more, drawn to the schooner 'Allie H. Belden,' which was aground just offshore. The vessel was engulfed by waves, with its crew clinging to the rigging. The surfmen quickly initiated a rescue attempt, employing the beach-apparatus [breeches buoy].

Despite the gale's fury, the first line reached the captain, who struggled to hold it and ultimately lost it to the wind. Subsequent attempts with another line failed as well. It became clear that a boat was the only means of saving the crew, despite the seemingly insurmountable challenge of launching one through the fierce surf.

By then, a crowd had gathered, eager to assist. With their help, the surfmen managed to launch the self-bailing surfboat. However, it was pushed back by the waves. Undeterred, the station crew and two volunteers took their boat, wading into the water and eventually breaking through the surf. Exhausted, they paused to regain their strength before continuing.

Through a combination of rowing, anchoring, and determination, the lifesavers finally reached the wreck after nine grueling hours. They rescued the captain, mate, and two seamen, all of whom were frostbitten and nearly spent after clinging to the shrouds for twelve hours. Tragically, two crew members had succumbed to the cold and fallen overboard.

The survivors were quickly taken to the station, where Dr. Hall of Lewes provided care, as noted in the 1888 'Annual Report of the US Lifesaving Service'. *Breeches buoy illustration collection National Archives*

Page 59 Michael Pupin, mule driver and beyond

Michael Pupin is acknowledged as one of the founding figures of the National Advisory Committee for Aeronautics, the precursor to NASA. His numerous patents include one that significantly extended long-distance telephone communication, which AT&T quickly acquired.

But his beginnings were humble. In his autobiography, "From Immigrant to Inventor," awarded the Pulitzer Prize for Literature in 1924, Pupin eloquently recounts his initial American mule driving experience:

"One of the farm hands, a Swiss, came in after a while in order to remind me that it was bedtime," he writes at the end of his long first day, "and to inform me that early in the morning he would wake me up and take me to the barn, where my job would be assigned to me. He kept his word, and with lantern in hand he took me long before sunrise and introduced me to two mules which he put in my charge.

"I cleaned them and fed them while he watched and directed; after breakfast he showed me how to harness and hitch them up. I took my turn in the line of teams hauling manure to the fields. He warned me not to apply myself too zealously to the work of loading and unloading, until I had become gradually broken in, otherwise I should be laid up stiff as a rod. The next day I was laid up, stiffer than a rod. He was much provoked and called me the worst greenhorn that he ever saw. But, thanks to the skilled and tender care of the ladies on the farm, I was at my job again two days later."

Over the next five years, Michael Pupin worked various farm jobs, eventually making his way north to New York City. He studied at night, working factory day jobs, to prepare for admission to Columbia University. Pupin landed a scholarship in 1879 and never looked back. The former mule driver successfully cast off his own bit and bridle to become one of the most innovative scientists of the age. *Mule illustration collection Smithsonian Institution*

Page 60 L.D. Caulk Dental Laboratories

Levin D. Caulk's efforts popularized the use of amalgam in American dentistry, revolutionizing dental practice.

Born in Camden in 1841, Caulk began his dental practice in Wilmington before moving to St. Louis, where he taught and practiced. Eventually, he returned to Camden and pivoted towards the manufacturing of dental products. In 1877, he established the L.D. Caulk Dental Depot, working out of his home and producing tooth cleansers.

Caulk moved his base to Milford and expanded as the L.D. Caulk Company in 1885. He began manufacturing tooth-filling materials such as gutta-percha (purified, coagulated latex from Malaysian Palaquium trees), amalgam (a paste made from mercury and silver), and cement.

Horse and buggy fleets initially transported L.D. Caulk Company products to dental product retailers throughout the mid-Atlantic region.

Levin D. Caulk passed away at the relatively young age of 56 due to complications from pneumonia, triggered by a horse-riding accident. At the time of his death, his dental manufacturing supply company was still a regional enterprise. Not until deep into the 20th century did the company grow exponentially, and via several mergers, eventually became part of Dentsply-Sirona.

Today, the once humble, Camden-based company has grown into the second-largest corporation in the worldwide dental equipment manufacturing sector. *Dental items, sign and Caulk home photo collection Milford Museum*

Page 61 Marydel Duel

The Gotham City rivals chose to battle out their differences on a tiny sliver of contested land just south of Marydel. The sleepy hamlet became the January 8, 1877 location for Delaware's last duel.

Marydel was easily accessible by railroad from Philadelphia. That Pennsylvania hub, in turn, was a central location for duelists traveling from major east coast locales. Marydel was, and still is, a quiet rural outpost far from the media or curious onlookers.

The advantageous attributes of this crossroads led James Gordon Bennett, publisher of the *New York Herald*, and Frederick May, a wealthy New York City socialite, to select Marydel for their showdown.

Bennett had been engaged to May's sister but broke off the contract and publicly spoke ill of her. This infuriated May, who felt his family's name had been tarnished. May started horsewhipping Bennett as he exited New York's Union Club one evening in early January. Bennett promptly challenged May to a duel. Both men, committed to defending their reputation, decided to face each other without further delay.

The contestants made their way separately to the appointed patch of frozen Delaware land, and the standoff ensued. Bennett managed to inflict a minor wound on May's arm, and the two combatants considered their honor restored. Neither faced legal consequences, as no witnesses were present aside from each man's "seconds" (attendants). Bennett and May departed Marydel on different trains and never again spoke to each other. *Pistol photo: Gift of William K. du Pont, Courtesy of Winterthur Museum, Garden & Library*

Page 62 Howard Pyle's Robin Hood

Howard Pyle's work extends well beyond his renowned interpretation of Robin Hood. In his vivid illustrations and narratives, he encapsulates the essence of lifelike tales. His plethora of expressive images feature American heroes, medieval adventurers, bold explorers, and pirates, all brimming with an irresistible blend of drama and emotion.

His influential "Book of Pirates" (1903) is a testament to Pyle's profound impact on pirate portaits. Pyle imbues his depiction with a remarkable attention to detail and dash of romanticism. The reader sees these seafaring outlaws not as brutal marauders, but as audacious, gallant adventurers. Pirates in Pyle's realm don an iconic garb of tricorn hats, sashes, earrings, and cutlasses - an ensemble that has since become synonymous with pirate imagery. This portrayal has permeated movies, literature, and even popular Halloween costumes.

Howard Pyle ardently shared his exceptional talent for narrative illustration with a multitude of students. His meticulous draftsmanship not only set the standard but also inspired generations of illustrators. Pyle's influence can be discerned in the works of noted artists such as N. C. Wyeth, Frank Schoonover, and Jessie Wilcox Smith.

Though Howard Pyle authored several immensely popular novels, his primary identity remains that of an illustrator. His artwork is renowned for its transformative impact on children's literature and visual American culture. Moreover, this collective body of works occupies a distinguished position in the annals of American art history and the esteem of Pyle's contemporaries.

Even Vincent van Gogh expressed his admiration for Howard Pyle's work, saying in a letter to his brother, "Do you know an American Magazine, Harper's Monthly? There are wonderful sketches in it … which struck me dumb with admiration … by Pyles." *Photo of Howard Pyle's easel and stool: Howard Pyle Manuscript Collection, Helen Farr Sloan Library & Archives, Delaware Art Museum, Gift of Anne Poole Pyle, 1923*

Page 63 Suffragist Mabel Vernon

The Wilmington native had already been active nationally in the suffrage movement for a decade. Her Swarthmore College friend Alice Paul, a leader in the crusade, convinced her to quit teaching high-school German and join the cause. At 23, Vernon's speaking and fund-raising skills helped her organize the Delaware headquarters of the Congressional Union for Woman Suffrage, which later became the National Woman's Party.

Vernon's 1916 presence at Wilson's speech was not her first time in Washington, DC advocating for suffrage. She organized a protest caravan in July 1913 from Wayne, PA to the Capitol. Groups from across the country converged to petition the Senate to act immediately on a proposed constitutional amendment granting women the right to vote. To garner support and interest, Vernon in late June led a 'Votes for Women' "roller chair" [wheelchair] parade along the Atlantic City boardwalk.

"Flying banners and pennants of Suffrage yellow will add to the brilliance of the march," said the *Evening Journal* [Wilmington], "besides having the effect much desired by the enthusiasts—namely, attracting public attention to the suffrage activities they are eager to initiate in Atlantic City and all the New Jersey resorts."

Mabel Vernon attracted a large crowd at the end of the parade. "We assume," she declared to her listeners, "that woman suffrage is bound to come; the thing we are concerned with is how soon, and as the quickest way is an amendment to the Federal constitution, that is what we are working for."

A local police officer approached her.

"We never have any kind of meetings on the boardwalk here," he informed Vernon, as reported by the *Washington Post*, "and therefore you will have to stop."

"But I have a permit from Mayor Riddle, and I will not stop," she replied.

The officer stated that if anyone in the crowd wanted her to stop, he would be obliged to disregard the permit. He then asked the crowd if anyone objected to her speaking.

"A small, wizened man said he objected," the *Post* reported, "and the policeman told her to stop. But she appealed to the crowd, and they shouted for her to go on in such a manner that the policeman and the small man beat a hasty retreat."

"But I followed the policeman, and got him to sign my petition," Vernon told the *Washington Post*.

The Delaware Chapter of the National Organization for Women presented Mabel Vernon late in life (1883-1975), with a citation as "one of the heroic foremothers of the movement to liberate women from the shackles of male chauvinism."

Vernon's response was characteristic. "Finish up on the Equal Rights Amendment," she told a NOW representative, "just as we had to come in and finish the fight for the national suffrage amendment. I'm proud my native state has already approved it." *Mannequin photo: Outfit of Leah Burton Paynter, collection Lewes History Museum; Mabel Vernon photo Library of Congress*

Page 64 Drowned at sea—twice

"A Mystery of the Sea," declared the *Daily Republican* [Wilmington] on page one of its August 20, 1884 edition. The paper explained that Captain Murray of the schooner 'Amy Schoolcraft' discovered a corked bottle floating off Cape Henry, VA containing several letters, "one of which was addressed to a lady of this city."

"This will let you know," the letter to her began, "that we were run into last night, June 20, by a large ocean steamer. The steamer tore away our forerigging, bowsprit, etc, and as soon as the bowsprit went both masts went with it. The steamer never stopped, but kept on her course. We judge we were about thirty miles southeast of Fenwick Island lighthouse, or 100 miles east of Cape May Point. The captain got excited and said the only thing to save us was to take to the boat and start for the shore. There was a heavy sea and the wind northwest...

... "George T. Nicholson"

"The other letter," continued the *Daily Republican*, "was to Nicholson's father, and is to the same effect."

"George T. Nicholson was well known in this city, where he was engaged in the commission business at No. 423 King St. until last February when he relinquished it to enter the wholesale commission house of Pattison & Company, in Baltimore. Some of his acquaintances seem to think that the whole affair is a canard."

A canard, eh?

"This story is a hoax," responded Frank A. Pattison of Pattison & Co the following day in the *Baltimore Sun*. "I received a letter from Nicholson less than one week ago, from Richmond, VA." Pattison told the *Sun* that Nicholson was never employed by his firm. "I can't conceive why he ever concocted such a story. You can take it for granted, however, that it is bogus from beginning to end."

"No such wreck as the one reported has been heard of, and no such vessel as the William Hazel is in the shipping lists," concluded the *Baltimore Sun*. Why didn't the newspaper seek out George Nicholson himself for comment? He is not on public record anywhere during

1884. He never came forward to explain the situation. But why would he be in touch with Pattison at all if he was on the run?

A George T. Nicholson appears for the first time in Baltimore's 1885 'Register of the Corporation Officers of Baltimore City' as an assistant clerk of Lexington Market and is in the Baltimore City Directories of 1886, 1887, 1888, 1889 in that same job capacity.

The story becomes murky, as another George T. Nicholson resides in Baltimore during the same period. That Nicholson was listed in the 1880 census as a bartender. It is possible Nicholson #2 switched jobs and became the clerk at Lexington Market. The 1890 census might have clarified that better, but it was mostly destroyed in two separate fires.

In 1890, one of the Georges applied for a building permit with Baltimore's Inspector of Buildings to add a shed to his property. Nicholson #2 passed away in 1892. Afterward, the story took yet another strange turn.

An intriguing coincidence arises from a February 15, 1894 news item in the *Delaware Gazette and State Journal*, which bears striking similarities to the 1884 "lost at sea" story. The 1894 piece reads:

"Baltimore, MD Feb 10 1894: The schooner 'Samuel H. Walker' departed Baltimore on December 15th, bound for Weymouth, near Fall River, Mass. Since then, nothing has been heard of the vessel. All hope for her safety has been abandoned, and she is presumed lost.

"The Walker was commanded by Captain George T. Nicholson, a resident of Wilmington, Delaware. In addition to her captain, she carried a crew of nine men. No trace of the vessel or crew has been discovered. The passage to Fall River typically takes a week. Laden with 931 tons of coal, the Walker was owned by S. H. Walker of Taunton, Mass."

The article concludes with a disclaimer from the paper's editor: "(The 'Samuel H. Walker' is not known in this city, nor does the name of Captain George T. Nicholson appear in the city directory. The statement that he resided in Wilmington, Del. is evidently a mistake —Ed. E.E.)"

Ladies and gentlemen, George T. Nicholson. *Drowning man illustration collection of Smithsonian Institution*

Page 65 'We Shall Overcome' origins

Charles A. Tindley was a determined soul. He blazed a remarkable trail into the Methodist ministry, all without the privilege of a formal education. Tindley actively taught himself to read and write by fireside, sounding out letters and eventually words. He poured himself into studying the Bible extensively.

Tindley gained freedom from slavery after the Civil War and relocated from his childhood home in Berlin, MD to Philadelphia. There, he found work as a janitor at the Calvary Methodist Episcopal Church. Later, he took divinity correspondence courses to further his understanding.

Tindley's relentless dedication and hard work did not go unnoticed by the church's leaders. Seeing his potential, the elders began to suggest him as a substitute preacher and encouraged him in his self-guided studies. In recognition of his efforts and extraordinary capabilities, the Methodist Episcopal Church (MEC) officially ordained him as Reverend Tindley in 1885.

The charismatic preacher devoted himself during his prime years from 1885 to 1902 by serving Methodist churches across the Delmarva region. His exceptional leadership in the Wilmington district caught the attention of the MEC, which honored him in 1899 with the title of presiding elder.

Tindley released "New Songs of the Gospel" in 1900, where the song "I'll Overcome Some Day" first appeared. Drawing inspiration from Galatians 6:9, this hymn assured early Christians that their virtuous deeds would eventually reap rewards.

Reverend Charles A. Tindley contributed 47 hymns to the world, six of which remain in The United Methodist Hymnal.

Page 66 Single Tax Orators arrested

Well-heeled landowners in Dover, along with their political allies, did not appreciate a tax movement hostile to their worldview recruiting converts in the vicinity.

The would-be stump speakers called themselves 'Georgists' after Henry George, a best-selling author and economist who ignited the single tax movement in the 1870s. George advocated for a significant shift in taxation. He envisioned a single flat tax, calculated at regular intervals, on a given parcel of land's highest potential value rather than on its current value, determined by income or property improvements.

This potential future wealth tax alarmed land developers, wealthy landowners, and industrialists. They feared high upfront tax obligations before the development or sale of land that currently had low value.

Supporters of George's theory sought to apply his ideas in a real-world scenario. A.H. Stevenson, a wealthy Philadelphia manufacturer, established the Philadelphia Single Tax Society (PSTS) and aimed to introduce a referendum in Delaware for the 1896 presidential election. Delaware, being near Philadelphia and small enough for speakers to thoroughly spread the message, seemed ideal for this experiment.

Upon arriving in Dover, Stevenson requested permission from Mayor Fisher to hold a rally along a main thoroughfare. The mayor suggested using The Green, an older and less populated part of town. Instead, Stevenson proceeded with his original plan, believing in his right to free speech, and was promptly arrested by Fisher for "noisy assemblage."

The PSTS continued sending an ongoing procession of 12 more speakers to Dover, each one promptly arrested by local law enforcement. Eventually, Governor William Watson intervened. The town released Stevenson and his supporters without further explanation.

The 1897 Delaware Constitutional Convention incorporated Section 7 of Article VIII, actively addressing real estate assessments and the inclusion of property values. The convention aimed to proactively prevent the implementation of any taxation system that could potentially result in land confiscation. "Let us speak out... against the ravages of those who entertain these new fancies," declared convention president John Biggs. He urged strong language, which would later become the force of law. It would protect Delaware from those seeking to experiment with new taxation systems at the state's expense. Biggs emphasized that these individuals "want to make their tests here, for the rest of the people of the United States."

Arden, DE holds a unique place in the history of Henry George's single tax movement. Founders Frank Stephens and Will Price designed Arden so that the 162-acre parcel was owned collectively by the village, and people could lease plots for their homes and businesses. The leaseholders would then pay a single tax on the land, which was intended to cover the costs of running the community, such as maintaining public spaces and roads. This model was meant to demonstrate the practicality of George's theories and offer a mold for wider implementation.

Arden emerged as a thriving colony for artists, writers, and thinkers. This in-state haven still operates today under a variation of the original single-tax leasehold system. New Castle's experimental hamlet stands as one of the most tangible realizations of Henry George's idea.
Man with megaphone photo: National Automotive History Collection / Glidden Collection / Detroit Public Library

Page 67 Chocolate murder by mail

The Commons, or The Green, played a crucial role in medieval life where villagers had access to common grazing land. Dover Green has considerably evolved from these humble origins. The town square is now characterized by its well-kept elms, maples, and sycamores. These trees act as a lush umbrella over a meticulously groomed carpet of bluegrass, presenting a miniaturized version of yesteryear's pastoral settings.

The idyllic space still functions as the town's heart. Summer concerts, Christmas caroling, autumn market fairs, and spring maypole dances take place here. The old State House, Biggs Museum, modern court, and stately homes of Delaware's first families surround The Green.

One of those mansions was built by Delaware congressman John Brown Pennington. His daughter, Mary, married newspaper reporter John P. Dunning in 1891. They moved to San Francisco with their baby daughter, where Dunning began an affair with Cordelia Botkin. When Mary discovered her husband's infidelity, she returned to her father's house on The Green.

John Dunning went to Cuba with the Spanish-American War's onset to cover the conflict, ended his affair with Cordelia, and planned to reconcile with Mary. A furious Cordelia plotted sweet revenge. Mary Dunning was enjoying a family gathering at her father's house when she received a box of chocolates with a note signed "Mrs. C." Assuming it was from a friend, she shared the candies with her guests.

That night, most attendees fell violently ill with severe stomach pains and vomiting. While most recovered, Mary Dunning and her sister, Ida, perished. A chemist found the remaining candies laced with arsenic. When Dunning returned from the war and saw the note, he immediately identified the culprit as his ex-paramour Cordelia.

Page 68 Death of a baby girl

Isaac Jacob Benioff, born in Kyiv, Ukraine, around 1840, learned the retail fur trade at 12, later married, and had four sons. The Benioff family immigrated to New York City in 1886, escaping Russian pogroms. Isaac went to work as an itinerant tailor, carrying his sewing machine from customer to customer. When Isaac, and his wife, Annie, had two more children, he returned to the stability of retailing and opened a fur store.

Following his first wife's death in 1894, Isaac married Ida, another Russian immigrant. Their first child, Sarah, who was born in 1896, suffered health issues from birth. Meanwhile, the Jewish Agriculture Society of NYC, underwritten by the railroads, began promoting low-cost loans to populate stops along new railroad lines. The Benioffs saw this "back to the soil" movement as an opportunity to rear Sarah in a healthier environment.

So, in 1897, Ida and the children moved from NYC to a farm in Viola, DE. Isaac continued working out of his West 14th Street shop. It was here that he encountered an experience that would leave him reeling - the shock of his lifetime.

"Upon the breast of the dead child was a note from his wife," reported an *Associated Press* dispatch picked up far and wide. "She wrote that she had been unable to find a Jewish cemetery at Viola and had accordingly sent the body to New York. The little corpse is now at the morgue, and because it was shipped in from another State there may be complications before a death certificate can be issued." The whereabouts of Sarah's remains, to this day, are unknown.

In 1914, Isaac, Ida, and the at-home children moved permanently to Allentown, PA, marking 17 years since they had put roots down in Delaware. *Woman's mourning bonnet collection Knowles Museum; child's coffin collection Harrington Historical Society*

Page 69 Victor Talking Machine and RCA

The primary photo illustrates a spring-wound motor. It supplies the mechanical energy needed to rotate the turntable at a consistent speed. The inset photo displays a reproducer, or sound box, which transforms the needles' mechanical vibrations into sound.

These were fundamental components in other phonographs around the turn of the century. Nevertheless, competitors lacked the relentless pursuit of perfection exemplified by Eldridge Johnson. A skilled engineer, Johnson spent years refining the design of his talking machine. The Victor Talking Machine Company founder debuted the Type B model in 1901.

Johnson's key insight was to perfect the governor of his spring motor. His innovation ensured a record's constant pitch during its playback. Inferior machines with poorly designed governors often produced uneven tones. Additionally, Johnson introduced wax master disks to the sound recording process. The breakthrough significantly improved sound quality and the overall recording process as compared to previous master disk technology.

Once Johnson launched his company, he started signing recording artists to exclusive contracts, including some of the most prestigious performers. Renowned opera tenor Enrico Caruso and popular American singer Jimmy Rodgers, for example, were featured on Victor Record's Red Seal. This star-studded strategy allowed Victor to establish a unique catalog of talent, setting their records apart from competitors. Exclusive contracts fostered artist-label associations, bolstering brand recognition and customer loyalty.

Eldridge Johnson, of Wilmington, was merely a pre-teen in 1878 when Thomas Edison invented the first phonograph. He studied at Newark's Delaware Academy. One year later, in 1883, the 16-year-old graduate began his apprenticeship at J. Lodge and Son, a machine repair shop in Philadelphia.

This training led Johnson to accept a machinist position at the Scull Machine Shop in Camden, NJ. He rose quickly to become foreman and manager but soon felt restless.

Johnson headed toward Washington State, vagabonding in search of fortune. Returning in 1894, he bought out the Scull Machine Shop and rebranded his acquisition the Eldridge Johnson Manufacturing Company. One day, a customer named Henry Whitaker came in with a question about a Berliner Gramophone.

German-born Emile Berliner emigrated to America in 1870. He initially survived with various odd jobs, but a hobby fiddling with inventions led him to experiment with sound recording and reproduction methods. He was granted a patent in 1887 for a Gramophone, the first of many inventions.

In 1894, Berliner and other entrepreneurs established the United States Gramophone Company. However, the group's seven-inch records still needed a hand-propelled machine. That year, Henry Whitaker requested Eldridge Johnson to design a spring-wound motor for the Berliner Gramophone. Johnson's company succeeded in 1895 and agreed to mass-produce motors for Berliner's enterprise. Johnson continued refining the design by externalizing the motor and incorporating a triple-based ball, ensuring a constant speed on the Berliner Gramophone.

Johnson spent the winter of 1896 in Philadelphia, where he met Alfred C. Clark. Clark had worked at Thomas Edison's first studio, then moved on to manage Berliner Gramophone's Philadelphia offices. Johnson collaborated with Clark on various Gramophone refinements, including an improved soundbox. The Clark-Johnson soundbox of 1897 became the foundation for Berliner's Improved Gramophone. Over the next three years, Johnson plunged ahead, secretly experimenting with recording and disc duplicating technologies.

Meanwhile, Berliner had established an exclusive partnership for US distribution with National Gramophone. Unbeknownst to Berliner, Frank Seaman, the president of National Gramophone, had illicitly founded a separate company called Universal Talking Machine. Berliner caught Seaman red-handed, marketing his own phonograph, the Zonophone. Furious at Seaman's double-dealing, Berliner cut off National Gramophone.

An awkward scenario escalated. Seaman sued Berliner Gramophone for breach of contract. Berliner then tried to protect his assets by merging with United States Gramophone. In response, Seaman sought an injunction to prevent the alliance. To counter this lawsuit, Berliner transferred his company patents to Johnson's newly established Consolidated Talking Machine in 1900.

The bitter legal dispute between Johnson, Berliner, and their former partner Frank Seaman resolved in Johnson's favor, and on March 12, 1901 he registered the 'Victor' trademark to avoid using the word 'Gramophone.'

Johnson broke ties with Berliner and restructured Consolidated Talking Machine as the Victor Talking Machine Company that same year. He then built the factory in Camden, NJ to avoid potential legal issues in Philadelphia. His name choice, "Victor," then, signified "Winner."

Ironically, Johnson acquired Frank Seaman's Universal Talking Machine Company assets in 1904 after the Zonophone's failure in the market.

Johnson went on to develop his business into the leading American producer of phonograph records, which subsequently achieved worldwide recognition. Victor was the corporate predecessor of what became RCA Records.

Emile Berliner and Eldridge Johnson both played crucial roles in the development of sound recording and reproduction technologies. Berliner's Gramophone invention, followed by Johnson's insights on spring-wound motors and soundboxes, laid the groundwork for future advancements in the music industry. Their legacies continue to shape the world of audio technology and have made a lasting impact on how people around the globe enjoy music. *Victrola components courtesy Johnson Victrola Museum*

Page 70 First RFD in Delaware

In July 1898, the *News Journal* reported that 107,062 Delawareans lacked free mail delivery, except for the experimental rural free delivery (RFD) services available in some areas. At the time, RFD was untested and faced opposition.

Fourth-class post offices, for instance, where postmasters were paid on commission, feared that RFD would result in their discontinuation. Congressmen were concerned about losing the limited patronage they had. Special Agent A.B. Smith of the new RFD Eastern Division explained that the service was initially meant to supplement existing fourth-class post offices in sparsely populated regions. Many postmasters found their roles to be unprofitable and annoying, but they opposed RFD when it threatened their positions.

Farmers worried about the financial burden of RFD, which required them to purchase standardized mailboxes and maintain local roads. Assistant Postmaster General Perry S. Heath tried to garner support from state grange associations and leading citizens to alleviate these concerns. He planned to test RFD in Harrington, Delaware, and possibly other locations.

The Harrington route began on October 3, 1898, initially covering 12.5 square miles and later extending to 18. Carrier Joseph G. Peckman served 100 people, a number that grew to 600 within a year and a half. Each carrier provided their horse and wagon and was exempt from road tolls.

By March 1900, RFD had expanded to other towns, with Marshallton handling Delaware's largest RFD mail volume. The service's popularity continued to grow, and by 1901, A.B. Smith declared in a report that RFD "diffuses intelligence, increases the volume of mail, promotes sociability, and tends to more exalted ideas of government." The experimental phase of RFD had come to an end. *Leather satchel collection Milford Museum; RFD buggy collection Marvel Carriage Museum; wooden mailbox ca. 1896-1900 collection /US Postal Museum/Smithsonian Institution; historical photo Delaware Public Archives*

Page 71 Delaware Corporate Tax Law first passed

The 'internal affairs doctrine' of corporate law states that a corporation's internal affairs should be governed by the laws of the state in which it is incorporated. Companies choosing to incorporate in the First State, then, know that their internal disputes will be promptly settled under the expert jurisprudence of Delaware's Court of Chancery.

Delaware's corporate law features did not emerge by chance. Samuel Arsht's "A History of Delaware Corporate Law" provides historical context. Between 1898 and 1899, a group of lawyers and politicians, "the group," saw the lucrative potential of attracting businesses to incorporate in Delaware.

"The group" is credited by Arsht with establishing the 1899 General Corporation Law. Arsht suggests they were inspired by an unpublished, undated thesis titled "The Development of the Delaware Corporation Law." James L. Wolcott wrote and submitted this piece to the Harvard Graduate School of Business Administration.

Wolcott, a Dover native and Chancery Court Chancellor from 1892 to 1895, passed away unexpectedly from a stroke in March 1898, at age 56. A year later, "the group" incorporated Corporation Trust Company of Delaware (CTC), implementing the General Corporation Law ideas Wolcott had laid out in his thesis.

James H. Hughes, Delaware Secretary of State from 1897 to 1901, had a significant role in shaping the General Corporation Law. He had been a law student under Wolcott prior to the latter's Chancery term.

The *Steubenville [OH] Herald-Star* identified the remaining members of "the group" in November 1900 as ex-Governor William T. Watson, W.H. Stayton, George Gray, and William M. Ross. Watson and Stayton respectively held the president and vice president roles at the CTC.

Former US Senator Gray and former Delaware State Treasurer Ross served as CTC directors. Hughes, then Delaware Secretary of State, acted as CTC counsel, representing 500+ Delaware-chartered corporations operating elsewhere.

Page 72 Christmas Seals

Wilmington newspapers frequently reported high TB death rates in workhouses and prisons. Class prejudice against this infected community was just one hindrance against efforts to eradicate TB. Furthermore, a cure remained unavailable, and the discovery of antibiotics was still over two decades away.

Wilmington's medical community formed the Anti-Tuberculosis Society (ATS) in the summer of 1906 to raise public awareness. Doctors believed that the best way to treat TB was to isolate patients and provide them with ample fresh air, no matter the outside temperature. In June 1907, the ATS began constructing "shacks" in Brandywine Hundred. They initially aimed to ward off and care for 10 patients.

The Brandywine Shacks relied entirely on private donations, as Wilmington's city council had not yet declared TB a public health crisis. Limited funding forced ATS to build the shacks with cheaper materials. Furthermore, the doctors warned they would abandon the project without public support.

The shacks quickly filled up despite the challenges. More space was needed, though. Fundraising efforts such as bake sales simply weren't enough to cover costs. The ATS considered admitting patients for free. Finally, the Delaware Branch of the American National Red Cross Society resolved the impasse by offering to collaborate with the ATS.

Wilmingtonian Emily Bissell, local Red Cross secretary, had a personal connection to the TB cause—her cousin Dr. John Wales was the sanatorium's director.

Bissell urged the sale of one-cent Red Cross Christmas Seal stamps at Wilmington post offices. The campaign idea, once approved, encouraged even the poorest citizens to contribute to the fight against TB. Wilmington's first year stamp sales totaled over $3,000. Next year's national campaign netted over $100,000. The movement's momentum coalesced around Emily Bissell.

Apart from her tireless work against TB, this American social activist took a unique stance on the issue of women's rights. Surprisingly, Bissell became a leader in the Anti-Suffrage camp. She opposed women's right to vote, believing that politics was a corrupting influence. Suffrage campaigns, she felt, interfered with women's philanthropic and social reform efforts.

Emily Bissell dedicated the rest of her life to the anti-tuberculosis movement and the ongoing Christmas Seal campaign. In recognition of her tremendous contributions, the US Postal Service honored her with a stamp in 1980. *Emily Bissell portrait collection United States Postal Service*

Page 73 Whipping post

The Allman Brothers Band's debut album in 1969 featured the iconic song "Whipping Post." This raw and impassioned track might lead listeners to envision a distant, more brutal era in American history. However, Delaware continued to legally permit the use of the whipping post for three years beyond the release of that song, only banning it in 1972. The First State, then, holds the dubious distinction of being the last state to outlaw this antiquated method of punishment. Furthermore, the pillory, out of use in most states by 1839, was only abolished by Delaware Governor Preston Lea in March 1905.

Pillories and whipping posts served as instruments of punishment in all three Delaware counties from 1717 forward. Their use was quite prevalent during the 18th century. As the 20th century arrived, however, Delaware's continued use of the two appeared increasingly archaic. For example, a 1912 case in which a horse thief received 30 lashes one week and another 30 the next, sparked a nationwide debate about Delaware's excessive whipping post usage.

The US House sponsored a resolution in response, seeking to eradicate Delaware's whipping punishments. They cited the 8th amendment's prohibition against cruel and unusual punishment as the grounds for their intervention. Despite this, Franklin Brockson, a Delaware representative, staunchly defended his state's practice. He recommended that members of the House instead turn their attention to their own affairs.

Several decades later, in 1935, *The Philadelphia Enquirer* published a graphic photograph of a Delaware whipping. After the image was reprinted nationwide, it became fodder for editorial cartoonists across the country. This prompted Delaware to act, passing a law that prohibited the photographing of such events.

Finally, on July 6, 1972, Governor Russell Peterson formally abolished whipping post usage, thus bringing a long overdue end to a harsh punishment era.

Page 74 Teddy Bears' Picnic

Bratton had already gained renown for his sentimental child ballads from the 1890s long before he composed 'The Teddy Bear Two-Step'. His 1894 song 'Only Me' poignantly depicted a mother's unequal treatment of her children, a theme still resonating with audiences. Bratton's relationship with his mother remains unknown, but the emotional depth in the composer's ballads suggests a complex personal history.

Bratton teamed up with lyricist Walter H. Ford, and the two produced around 100 hits during the Gay Nineties. Vocalist Ethel Woods contributed early lyrics to "The Teddy Bear Two-Step," originally a piano instrumental. London lyricist Jimmy Kennedy later replaced her words with his timeless lines:

If you go out in the woods today
You're sure of a big surprise.
If you go out in the woods today
You'd better go in disguise.

Henry Hall's Orchestra recorded Kennedy's version of "The Teddy Bears Picnic" in 1932. Many more recording artists, including Bing Crosby, Rosemary Clooney, and Anne Murray have kept the tune alive. Likewise, television shows, films, and commercials right up to the present feature the ditty. John W. Bratton, the boy from New Castle who grew up with his grandmother, earned the title "grand old man of tin pan alley." He lived long enough to see his song become a classic before passing away in 1947 at the age of 80.

Page 75 Red Demons, Green Flyers, and Knock-a-Bouts

Du Pont's inaugural adventure with a gas-powered car ended in a breakdown in November 1900. By February of the following year, he was on to his third vehicle, a French-made Runabout from De Dion-Bouton. This car company may not be a familiar name today but held the title of the world's largest automobile manufacturer at that time. Wilmington's *Morning News* praised the car as a "neat machine." The Runabout's user-friendly operations required minimal physical strength, making the design particularly suited for women.

George K. Rudert, a Wilmington watchmaker, announced his intentions to build a steam-driven automobile in May 1901. That December, he proudly showcased his first model. Rudert continued to innovate, securing a patent for a unique steering device in 1906. However, by 1926, Rudert had returned to watchmaking, fading from the automotive industry's spotlight.

The *Smyrna Times* reported a proposed 'automobile line' between Lewes and Rehoboth in June 1901. The article announced plans for construction of the first road in Delaware dedicated specifically to car traffic.

The influential Alfred I. du Pont had a significant impact on fostering the acceptance of automobiles in Delaware. His impressive personal commitment to this technology was evident as he owned four automobiles by May 1902, inspiring widespread enthusiasm. As a result, public excitement led to vital infrastructure developments and a broader adoption of automobile use across the First State.

Cars became a common sight in Wilmington by April 1903, and manufacturers began diversifying their products. The same year, the "Good Roads" movement emerged, pushing for improved roadways. Delaware's General Assembly, in turn, allocated $30,000 to initiate road paving.

Wilmington's 'autoists' organized an automobile club in September 1904 to influence public policy on road construction and associated regulations. The following year, 1905, Delaware legislators introduced their first motor vehicle oversight. The registration enactment required an annual fee of $2 and an owner's license plate.

The concept of car dealerships materialized around 1906, with early dealers incorporating car sales into their primary business. However, fleet ownership was still years away from emerging. The postal service, for example, did not formalize shared vehicle inventory until the 1920s. Prior to that, individual postmen were expected to buy their own car. Joshua B. Gray, of Milton, was the first Delaware carrier to do so in 1907.

That same year marked a turning point in the state's automobile regulations. Delaware began issuing operator's licenses and taxing motorcars.

Alfred du Pont's cousin, Thomas Coleman du Pont financed the construction of the DuPont Highway, also known as Route 13, several years later. Since its inception in 1911, the pike has remained one of two major north-south arteries traversing the state.

This roadway, one of the first divided highways in the United States, has played—and continues to play—a significant role in the modernization and ongoing functionality of Delaware's transportation system. *Stanley Locomobile photo collection of Henry Ford Museum of American Innovation; car in mud photo Library of Congress*